D0402779

# CONSERVATISM

# CONSERVATISM

## *An Invitation to the Great Tradition*

**ROGER SCRUTON**

**ALL
POINTS
BOOKS**

www.stmartins.com

Designed by Jade Design

The Library of Congress Cataloging-in-Publication Data
is available upon request.

ISBN 978-1-250-17056-9 (hardcover)
ISBN 978-1-250-17073-6 (ebook)

Our books may be purchased in bulk for promotional, educational, or business use. Please contact your local bookseller or the Macmillan Corporate and Premium Sales Department at 1-800-221-7945, extension 5442, or by email at MacmillanSpecialMarkets@macmillan.com.

First published in Great Britain by Profile Books Ltd

First U.S. Edition: June 2018

10  9  8  7  6  5  4  3  2  1

# CONTENTS

PREFACE                                          1

1 PRE-HISTORY                                    9

2 THE BIRTH OF PHILOSOPHICAL
  CONSERVATISM                                   33

3 CONSERVATISM IN GERMANY
  AND FRANCE                                     55

4 CULTURAL CONSERVATISM                          79

5 THE IMPACT OF SOCIALISM                       103

6 CONSERVATISM NOW                              127

  Further reading and bibliography             157

# CONSERVATISM

# PREFACE

We live at an important time in the history of the post-war conservative movement. Issues that were for years undiscussable have appeared at the top of the agenda, and demographic and strategic changes have redrawn the map of the world. The internet and the social media have disrupted the political process, bypassing the official filters in order to go straight to the target, which is a one-click response on a smartphone. In these circumstances we should not be surprised if people previously unimaginable as the holders of high office suddenly emerge at the top. Nor should we be surprised if the separation of powers has become the antagonism of powers, with the branches of government competing for the high ground of political influence.

Neither liberals nor conservatives were prepared for this, though it has given a new lease of life to the liberal worldview, with the media and the universities united against the 'populism' that has swept away the checks and balances of the political process. In this new situation conservatism inevitably has a beleaguered air, as the institutions, procedures and values on which it has relied one by one vanish into air. It is the right time, therefore, to look seriously at the *past* of conservatism, and to explore what its philosophical thinkers have been saying all along. As I explain in this book, conservatism emerged at the Enlightenment as a necessary counter to the excesses of liberal individualism, and its arguments are as valid and relevant today as they were when they first began to take shape in the seventeenth century.

It is undeniable, however, that conservatives have not, in recent times, always been clear as to the source of their beliefs, or the goals for which they should be striving. When I first became conscious of my own political leanings, conservatism defined itself in terms of the worldwide confrontation between freedom and totalitarianism. Of course there were nuances, disputes and alliances. Traditional conservatives and free-market libertarians were often at loggerheads, and there was and remains a deep dispute on the conservative side as to whether the sphere of culture is or is not a concern of government. Still, it was undeniable to anyone who had experience of both sides that this worldwide conflict existed, and that conservatism ended with the defence of free societies against the totalitarian project, even if it didn't begin there. Seeing things that way had the advantage of presenting conservatism as an international cause, something grander and more intimately connected with the future of mankind than the local attachments from which ordinary conservative sentiments tend to grow.

However, conservatism is not, by nature, an international cause. It takes its character from local questions, and the loves and suspicions that thrive in specific places and times. For conservatives all disputes over law, liberty and justice are addressed to a historic and existing community. The root of politics, they believe, is *settlement* – the motive in human beings that binds them to the place, the customs, the history and the people that are theirs. The language of politics is spoken in the first-person plural and the duty of the politician is to maintain that first-person plural in being. Without it law becomes an alien imposition, not *ours* but *theirs*, like the laws imposed by a conquering power, or those, as we have experienced in Britain, imposed by a treaty made years ago in a vanished situation by people long since dead. Conservatives are not reactionaries. As Burke said, 'we must reform in order to conserve', or, in more modern idiom: we must adapt. But we adapt to change in the name of continuity, in order to conserve what we are and what we have. The need to see things in this way is as strong today as it was at the American Founding, and the recent presidential election gave vivid proof that the question who we are now occupies the centre of political thinking.

Those who describe themselves as liberals tend to react to this question with suspicion. Identities, they argue, shift and morph. The 'we' of politics is never stable, and all boundaries are in essence negotiable. Hence there is only one cogent reaction to the global forces that impinge on us, which is to open our political thinking to the wider world. For liberals it is not the specifics of our local history and acquired obligations that should govern our political behaviour, but the universal ideals of the Enlightenment.

The conservative response to the liberal individualism of the Enlightenment has been to insist on the contingent and attached nature of the human individual. In our present circumstances this means insisting that governments are elected by a specific people in a specific place, and must meet the people's needs, including the most important of their needs, which is the need to trust their neighbours. That is why, in the current debates, conservatives are emphasizing the defence of the homeland, the maintenance of national borders, and the unity and integrity of the nation. And this is also a point of tension in conservatism, today as it has been in the past, since belief in a free economy and free trade inevitably clashes with local attachments and community protection.

In modern conditions, in which governments rarely enjoy a majority vote, most of us are living under a government of which we don't approve. We accept to be ruled by laws and decisions made by politicians with whom we disagree, and whom we perhaps deeply dislike. How is that possible? Why don't democracies constantly collapse, as people refuse to be governed by those they never voted for? Why do the protests of disenchanted voters crying 'not my president!' peter out, and why has there been after all no mass exodus of liberals to Canada?

The answer, conservatives argue, is that political communities, democracies included, are held together by something stronger than politics. There is a 'first person plural', a pre-political loyalty, which causes neighbours who voted in opposing ways to treat each other as fellow citizens, for whom the government is not 'mine' or 'yours' but 'ours', whether or not we approve of it. Many are the flaws in this system of government, but one feature gives it an insuperable advantage over all others so far devised, which is that it makes those who exercise power accountable to those who did not vote for them. This kind of accountability is possible only if the electorate is bound together as a 'we'. Only if this 'we' is in place can the people trust the politicians to look after their interests. Trust enables people to cooperate in ensuring that the legislative process is reversible, when it makes a mistake; it enables them to accept decisions that run counter to their individual desires and which express views of the nation and its future that they do not share. It is to the maintenance of that kind of trust that conservative politics has always been directed. Of course conservatives value liberty, and acknowledge the right of individuals to choose their own way to happiness. But they also believe that the human individual is an artefact, brought into being by the customs and institutions of society, and that true liberty arises only from a culture of obedience, in which law and community are shared assets maintained for the common good.

Hence it was in the name of their social and political inheritance that conservatives fixed their banner to the mast of freedom. What they meant was *this* kind of freedom, the freedom enshrined in our legal and political inheritance, and in the free associations through which our societies renew their legacy of trust. So understood freedom is the outcome of multiple agreements over time, under an over-arching rule of law. And the task of politics is to establish a 'constitution of liberty', as Hayek described it. Freedom is not a set of axioms but an evolving consensus. This consensus cannot be easily described. Sir Isaiah Berlin's famous distinction between negative and positive liberty does not capture the crucial idea of a free *community*, in which constraints are real, socially engendered, but also tacitly accepted as a part of citizenship. Nor is it the absence of domination that has been valued and assumed in Britain and the United States. What our two political communities have valued and protected is the harmony between public customs and private choices. We have lived by a tacit agreement to abide by norms that constrain our choices without coercing them. And we have agreed to this because for us freedom is a way of *belonging.*

Liberals are beneficiaries of this belonging. But they believe in the right of individuals and communities to define their identity for themselves, regardless of existing norms and customs. They do not see liberty as a shared culture, based in tacit conventions. On the left it is the negative that inspires. And a whole language has developed with which to abuse those who cling to the existing social order, the inherited hierarchies, the old and tried conventions. In the vociferous times in which we live this abusive language, accusing conservatives of 'racism', 'xenophobia', 'homophobia', 'sexism' – with an 'ism' or a 'phobia' to dismiss every aspect of our cultural capital – has made it hard for conservatives to speak out coherently, or even to catch their breath as they run from the noise. Nevertheless, their arguments need to be met by their opponents, and I have written this book in the hope of encouraging well-meaning liberals to take a look at what those arguments really are.

As I try to show, conservative thinking has never been devoted to freedom alone. Nor has the agenda been about economic freedom, important though that was during the debates and upheavals of the twentieth century. It has been about our whole way of being, as heirs to a great civilisation and a many-layered bequest of laws, institutions and high culture. For conservatives our law-governed society came

into being because we have known who we are, and defined
our identity not by our religion, our tribe or our race but by
our country, the sovereign territory in which we have built
the free form of life that we share. And if there is another
way of staying together in the world as it is today, I should
be interested to hear of it.

# 1

# PRE-HISTORY

Modern conservatism is a product of the Enlightenment. But it calls upon aspects of the human condition that can be witnessed in every civilisation and at every period of history. Moreover, it is heir to a philosophical legacy at least as old as the Greeks. Aristotle, in the *Politics,* defended constitutional government in terms that are as influential among conservative thinkers today as they were in the ancient world. Indeed, most of the ideas purveyed by modern conservatives are foreshadowed in Aristotle's great work. But they have been adapted to a situation that Aristotle himself could not have foreseen, which is the emergence of the nation state, the loss of a unifying religion, and the growth of the 'great society', composed of millions of cooperating strangers under a single rule of law.

It is a repeated error among intellectual historians to assume that ideas have a self-contained history of their own, and that one idea gives rise to another in something like the way one weather system gives rise to the next. Marxists, who regard ideas as by-products of economic forces, commit the opposite error, dismissing the intellectual life as entirely subservient to material causes. The vast and destructive influence of Marxist theory is a clear disproof of what it says. As the American conservative Richard Weaver put it, in the title of a famous and influential book,

*Ideas Have Consequences* (1948), and this is as true of conservative ideas as it is of ideas propagated on the left. To understand the pre-history of conservatism, therefore, one should accept that ideas have a far-reaching influence over human affairs; but one should recognise also that they do not arise only from other ideas, and often have roots in biological, social and political conditions that lie deeper than rational argument.

We human beings live naturally in communities, bound together by mutual trust. We have a need for a shared home, a place of safety where our claim to occupancy is undisputed and where we can call on others to assist us in times of threat. We need peace with our neighbours and the procedures for securing it. And we need the love and protection afforded by family life. To revise the human condition in any of those respects is to violate imperatives rooted in biology and in the needs of social reproduction. But to conduct political argument as though these factors are too far from the realm of ideas to deserve a mention is to ignore all the limits that must be borne in mind, if our political philosophy is to be remotely believable. It is precisely the character of modern utopias to ignore these limits – to imagine societies without law (Marx and Engels), without families (Laing), without borders or defences (Sartre).[1] And much

---

1   Friedrich Engels, *Anti-Dühring*, Part 3, Chapter 2, on the 'withering away of the State'; R. D. Laing, *The Politics of the Family*, London, 1971, decrying the 'bourgeois family' as the source of collective mental sickness; J.-P. Sartre, *Between Existentialism and Marxism*, translated by J. Matthews, London, 1974, arguing that all boundaries will dissolve after the 'totalising' revolution, when nations, classes, borders will be replaced by the constantly evolving '*groupe en fusion*'.

conservative ink has been wasted (by me among others) in rebutting such views, which can be believed only by people who are unable to perceive realities, and who therefore will never be persuaded by argument.

Let us begin, therefore, by listing some of the features of the human condition that define the limits of political thinking and that, most conservatives will claim, are given due prominence in their philosophy. First among these features is social membership. Human beings live in communities, and depend on communities for their safety and happiness. In a tribal society people relate to each other through kinship (which may be partly mythical); in a religious society membership is determined by ritual and faith; in a political society relations are governed by law, and in the modern secular state law is made by the citizens, usually through their elected representatives, and imposed by a sovereign authority. All three forms of society – tribal, religious and political – can be witnessed in the world today, though it was the emergence of political order that was the original inspiration for modern conservatism. On one reading of events, indeed, conservatism arose as an attempt to hold on to the values of kinship and religion in communities that were being reorganised by a purely political law.

Social membership goes hand in hand with individual attachment. Human beings begin life in a state of attachment to the mother and to the household that shields and nurtures her. As they grow to adulthood the bond of attachment loosens and widens. The young adult needs the mother and the family less, but friends and cooperation more. In the course of a lifetime customs, places, networks, institutions, shared ways of being all amplify our attachments, and create the sense that we are at home in the world, among familiar and trustworthy things. That sense of the familiar and the trustworthy is precious to us, and its loss is an occasion of anxiety and mourning. The most important input into conservative thinking is the desire to sustain the networks of familiarity and trust on which a community depends for its longevity. Conservatism is what its name says it is: the attempt to conserve the community that we have – not in every particular since, as Edmund Burke put it, 'we must reform in order to conserve', but in all matters that ensure our community's long-term survival.

But human beings do not only cooperate. They also compete, and it is a primary need, therefore, to ensure that competition is peaceful, and that conflicts can be resolved. Almost all the utopias that have been devised by modern writers are based on the assumption that human beings can exist in arrangements where cooperation alone binds people to their neighbours, and from which the element of competition has been refined away. And this is why utopias are unbelievable – being either purely abstract arrangements of noumenal beings, like the 'full communism' foretold by Marx and Engels in *The German Ideology* (1845), or sentimental fairylands, like the neo-Gothic England of William Morris's *News from Nowhere* (1890). Competition is fundamental to our nature, being both our way of solving problems, and the most important human cause of them. Kinship moderates competition, replacing 'I' by 'we' in all disputes that might spill over into violence. But it also creates rivalry between families, like the Montagues and

Capulets, and between tribes, like those brought to order by Muhammad, with the discovery of a religion that demanded 'submission', and therefore 'peace'. That religious 'peace' in turn meant war against the heretics and infidels.

In the modern world of the Enlightenment the old forms of social membership had run their course in a series of religious wars. People were searching for new ways of implanting reconciliation in the heart of the social order, and secular government under a rule of law seemed to be the best hope for the future, since it promised to put reason rather than passion in charge. The Enlightenment inspired the collective recognition that human beings had been fighting over fictions, and that it was time to agree about realities instead.

In the pre-history of conservative thinking, when Aristotle was the supreme master, it was usual to follow him in emphasising reason as distinctive of the human condition. By exercising our reason we have a unique means of resolving conflict and overcoming obstacles. But it was already apparent to Aristotle, and has been made explicit by modern studies in collective decision-making, that when a group of people all apply their reason to a shared problem, a reasonable solution may nevertheless not emerge – in other words, that the rational and the reasonable may diverge. This is shown clearly by the Prisoners' Dilemma, in which two prisoners, each choosing rationally, will act in a way that is counter to the best interests of both.[2] And it was a crucial observation of Burke's, in his polemic against

---

2  This is the starting point for a discussion of collective choice, and if you don't know what the Prisoners' Dilemma is you should consult one of a million references to it on the internet.

the French Revolution, that rational plans in the brains of ardent believers may lead of their own accord to disaster.

Conservatives tend to share Aristotle's conception of human rationality and, like him, recognise that one aim of political life is to refine the use of reason, and to implant in the citizen the virtues that are necessary for its collective exercise. But the point has been made differently at different times that we rational beings need customs and institutions that are founded in something other than reason, if we are to use our reason to good effect. This insight, indeed, is probably the principal contribution that conservatism has made to the self-understanding of the human species. In the following chapters I will spell it out in more detail.

That said, however, we should recognise the countervailing tendency in conservative thought. As well as emphasising the need for custom and community, conservative philosophy has advocated the freedom of the individual, conceiving community not as an organic network bound by habit and submission, but as a free association of rational beings, all of whom have, and cherish, an identity of their own. Conservatism as we know it today is a distinctively modern outlook, shaped by the Enlightenment and by the emergence of societies in which the 'we' of social membership is balanced at every point against the 'I' of individual ambition.

The idea of society as a collection of individuals, each with a sphere of autonomous choice and all pursuing personal fulfilment along a path of their own, is not a recent one. In a famous study, the Swiss historian Jacob Burckhardt attributed the emergence of the individual to the intellectual and political awakening of the Renaissance, while in a recent book, Sir Larry Siedentop has traced the idea further back, to the religion of Jesus and St Paul, which places the salvation of the individual soul at the heart of God's concern for us.[3] Whatever the truth of those views, it is surely evident that individualism took on a new character at the Enlightenment, with the emphasis on the connection between legitimacy and consent. The modern conception of political society, as an assembly of citizens who cooperate in establishing the laws under which they live, is to be distinguished from older ideas of monarchical sovereignty, qualified, in whatever way, by the need for the monarch to consult and conciliate the powerful groups within the kingdom.

But it should not be thought that the transition from that older idea to modern forms of parliamentary democracy is clear-cut and absolute. On the contrary, in the British case it has been established at least since the reign of Edward III (r. 1327–77) that the king cannot tax his subjects without consent of the House of Commons, and the subsequent history of the English Crown has revolved around the increasingly successful attempts of Parliament to gain control over important decisions. By the time of the Glorious Revolution of 1688, with the deposition of James II, the last Stuart king, in favour of William of Orange, and with the adoption by Parliament in 1689 of a Bill of Rights, it was clear that England had become a constitutional

3  Jacob Burckhardt, *The Civilization of the Renaissance in Italy*, 1860;
   Sir Larry Siedentop, *Inventing the Individual: The Origins of Western Liberalism*, 2014.

monarchy, in which the power of the monarch was limited by customs and conventions that transferred the main business of government to the two houses of Parliament.

It was at this time that the principal ideas behind the modern conservative movement began to emerge in both Britain and France, and some of these ideas were shared at first with the liberal individualists who were to provide the intellectual fuel for the French Revolution. The first and most far-reaching idea was that the legitimacy of a government depends on the consent of those who are subject to it. Authority is conferred on the government by the people, who are the ultimate source of sovereign power. This – to us obvious – idea involves a reversal of the medieval view of government, according to which the monarch, appointed by historical (which usually meant divine) right, is the source of all authority in the state. In the medieval view, the freedom of the individual is a privilege, conferred by the monarch in return for military or courtly services. Even if individualism was on the rise throughout the medieval period, it had yet to find expression in a philosophy, and theories of government saw legitimacy as flowing down to individuals from their sovereigns, and not, as was later accepted, flowing up to the sovereigns from those who consented to their rule.

At the same time, medieval discussions contain fruitful explorations of two issues that were to emerge as pivotal at the Enlightenment: the relation between ecclesiastical and secular government, and the limits to government contained in the law of nature. The Greek Stoics had argued that laws are of two kinds, man-made and 'natural'. The natural law owes its authority to our innate reasoning powers, and the existence of such a law was defended by the great scholastic philosopher St Thomas Aquinas (1226–1274), who saw it as providing a standard against which the justice of all merely human arrangements could be measured. Discussions of this went hand in hand with attempts both to circumscribe and to define the power of the church, and to reconcile the competing needs for an inclusive secular order and for sacred institutions devoted to the spiritual well-being of the community. The growing conflict between church and state at the Reformation, and the increasing emphasis on natural law as setting limits to the sovereign power, were powerful factors in displacing the medieval idea, that legitimacy flows downwards from the sovereign to the subject, and replacing it with the liberal view, that legitimacy flows upwards from the people to the sovereign power.

In one of the first works of political philosophy to be marked by the recognisable tone of voice of British conservatism, Richard Hooker (1554–1600), in *Of the Laws of Ecclesiastical Polity* (from 1594), attempted to justify a compromise between church and state. Each, Hooker believed, should limit the scope of the other, in the interests of the natural law that would guarantee the liberties of the individual and ensure peace between the spiritual and temporal powers.

That work, esteemed though it is by many conservatives today, belongs to the pre-modern period of political debate. The modern vision of legitimacy was first fully expressed in the English-speaking world by Thomas Hobbes (1588–1679), whose celebrated *Leviathan* (1651) attempts to derive an account of good government from the assumption that the 'commonwealth' is composed of freely choosing individuals, motivated by their beliefs and desires. In a state of nature, Hobbes argued, these appetite-driven individuals will be in competition for the resources needed to survive and prosper, and the result will be the war of all against all. In that condition, life will be, in his famous words, 'solitary, poor, nasty, brutish and short'. But individuals have the means to rise above the state of nature, since they make rational choices and agree with each other to act for their mutual benefit. Hence they will contract among themselves to establish a government, which will have sovereignty over them all and provide protection to each. The sovereign created by the social contract will not be party to the contract, but will enjoy the absolute power to enforce the contract against those who strive to bypass or renege on it.

The detail of Hobbes's theory need not concern us. What is important is the concept of sovereignty that he justified. It might be thought that a philosopher who sees the source of political authority as lying in the consent of the individual subject would end with a mild, flexible and negotiable idea of legitimate order. But not so. Hobbes had lived through the civil war and witnessed (from the safe distance of Paris) the profound disorder and cruelty that followed from the collapse of government. Anything was better than the chaos that he had observed, and if the absolute power of a sovereign is the only thing that can prevent it, then that is how things must be. Moreover, rational beings, understanding this, would sign up to the contract whereby the absolute sovereign is brought into being.

Immediately in the wake of Hobbes came *The Commonwealth of Oceana* (1656) by James Harrington (1611–77), which presented the picture of an ideal secular state. Harrington was an admirer of Machiavelli, whose cynical advice to secular rulers, *The Prince* (1532), had shocked the world with its realistic portrayal of political power. Harrington attempted to show that republican government in an essentially capitalist society – a 'commonwealth for increase' – would be the most stable political system. In the course of this he argued for a written constitution, bicameral government, secret ballots, the indirect election of a president and many other features of the ideal state, which was to be, in his famous words, 'an empire of laws, not of men'. Harrington's work, which was to exert a powerful influence upon many of the Founding Fathers of the US Constitution, followed Hobbes in decisively rejecting any suggestion that religious obedience, rather than popular consent, has a part to play in conferring legitimacy on a government.

The *Two Treatises of Civil Government* (1690) of John Locke (1632–1704) took the argument for popular sovereignty one step further. Locke, strongly influenced by Hooker, returned to the idea of a natural law. We understand this law, Locke suggested, not as an abstract imperative, but as an inner sense of our rights. There are natural rights, which are acknowledged by all reasoning beings. It is given to reason to perceive these rights, which exist independently of any social order. Principal among them are the rights to life, limb and freedom of action: no one can deprive me of these without doing me wrong, unless I myself have done something to give him just cause (perhaps not even then, if these rights are truly 'inalienable'). There is also a natural right to private property: any object which is appropriated or produced by 'mixing my labour' with it is, given certain conditions, mine, as much as the limbs that worked on it are mine.

Rational beings recognise those natural rights even in a state of nature, and do not require the absolute protection and control of Hobbes's sovereign to claim them against each other. They are specific individual rights and cannot be removed or limited except by the consent of those possessing them, a process which probably extends only to freedom of action and property, and not to life and limb, the rights to which are, in Locke's view, inalienable. All government, since it involves the limitation of the freedom of the subjects and their subjection to a higher power, must be the result of consent if it is to be legitimate, and no government is made legitimate in any other way. The model for legitimate government is therefore to be found in contract. The transition from the state of nature to the state of civil society would be legitimate were it to result from a social 'compact', by which free beings contract among each other to accept the curtailment of their rights in exchange for the benefits and security of society. This compact is not a historical event, but, as it were, a structure concealed within society, which is revealed by 'tacit consent'.

Civil society forms itself into particular institutions of government, which enshrine and protect the contractual relation among its members. Locke suggested that liberties could be better protected and the social compact better upheld by an effective separation of powers – thereby emphasising a notion, already introduced by Harrington, that was to have a radical influence on both liberal and conservative thinking, partly through the more careful and systematic theory of it given by Montesquieu.

Charles-Louis de Secondat, Baron de Montesquieu (1689–1755), admired Locke and the English constitution (or what he took to be the English constitution), praising it as 'the mirror of liberty'. His *Spirit of the Laws* (1734) contains the most influential version of the theory that the powers of government are exercised in three separate spheres – the executive, the legislative and the judicial – and that the spheres should be separated as far as possible in order to guarantee the liberties of the subject. Montesquieu argued that only an aristocratic government on the English model could create an effective balance of these powers within the state, avoiding the despotic tendencies inherent both in absolute monarchy and in government by the common people. He defended liberty, but his desire was more to restore old liberties that the absolutism of Louis XIV had eroded than to advocate the new liberties of the Enlightenment.

Harrington, Locke and Montesquieu all influenced the American Founders, who framed their constitution along the lines those thinkers suggested – with executive power vested in the president, legislative power in Congress and judicial power in the Supreme Court. And Montesquieu was admired by both liberals and conservatives in the aftermath of the Enlightenment, not least by the great conservative Edmund Burke, who praised him for what he took to be a thoroughgoing attempt to articulate the idea of liberty in terms of a conservative vision of social order. Although Locke and Montesquieu took the theory of liberal individualism forward in ways that gave support both to the American revolutionaries and to the far more radical French revolutionaries who followed them, their fundamental conceptions appear as much in the writings of conservatives as in those of liberals, and this point must be grasped if we are to understand exactly how modern conservatism arose and what, ultimately, it has stood for.

Locke's first *Treatise of Civil Government* was directed against a kind of conservatism – the *pre-modern* conservatism of Sir Robert Filmer (1588–1653), who had published a tract justifying the belief in a divine right of kings. Filmer's was a rearguard attempt to defend a rapidly deflating conception of civil government, one that had been fatally punctured by the civil war. Henceforth, the dispute between liberals and conservatives would emerge in its modern form, as a dispute within the broad ideas of popular sovereignty, the liberty of the individual, and constitutional rights. Although later, in the wake of the French Revolution, doubt was cast on those ideas, and a version of 'divine right' was reinstated by the great French polemicist Joseph de Maistre, this would now be regarded as a reactionary rather than a conservative development – that is, an invocation of an old order of things, rather than an invitation to adapt to changing circumstances in a spirit of conservation and renewal.

In the wake of Locke, the frontier between the liberal and the conservative position became a frontier *within* the domain of popular sovereignty, and we will understand modern conservatism as a political movement only if we see that some elements of liberal individualism have been programmed into it from the outset. In particular, conservatives and liberals agree on the need for limited government, representative institutions, the separation of powers, and the basic rights of the citizen, all of which must be defended, they both believe, against the top-down administration of the modern collectivist state.

This point is obscured by the fact that the term 'liberal' is now used in two conflicting ways, on the one hand to denote the politics and philosophy of individual liberty, as advocated by Locke and his followers, on the other hand to denote the 'progressive' ideas and policies that have emerged in the wake of modern socialism. In effect, the two ideas belong to two contrasting narratives of emancipation. Classical liberalism tells of the growth of individual liberty against the power of the sovereign. Socialism tells of the steadily increasing equality brought about by the state at the expense of the entrenched hierarchies of social power. The French revolutionaries went into battle with a slogan that promised liberty and equality together. Subsequent history might be taken to suggest that the goals are, in practice, incompatible, or at least in radical tension with each other. When considering the pre-history of conservatism it is important to note that it was initially a response to 'classical' liberalism, and one that incorporated many of Locke's core ideas, including the emphasis on natural rights, and the right of property.

Modern conservatism, therefore, began life in Britain and also in France as a *qualification* of liberal individualism.

The conservative argument accepted the bottom-up view of legitimacy, as conferred on government, at least in part, by the consent of the people. It accepted some version of natural law and natural rights, as defining the limits of political power and the freedoms of the sovereign individual. And it was by and large in favour of constitutional government and of what Jefferson was later to describe as 'checks and balances' (*Notes on the State of Virginia*, query XII), through which the various powers and offices of government could hold each other to account.

In all those ways modern conservatism arose as a defence of the individual against potential oppressors, and an endorsement of popular sovereignty. However, it opposed the view that political order is founded on a contract, as well as the parallel suggestion that the individual enjoys freedom, sovereignty and rights in a state of nature, and can throw off the burden of social and political membership, and start again from a condition of absolute freedom. For the conservative, human beings come into this world burdened by obligations, and subject to institutions and traditions that contain within them a precious inheritance of wisdom, without which the exercise of freedom is as likely to destroy human rights and entitlements as to enhance them.

The first great modern defender of that kind of conservatism in Britain was the judge Sir William Blackstone (1723–1780), whose *Commentaries on the Laws of England* (4 vols, 1765–69) set out to defend the English common law and unwritten constitution as concrete applications of the natural law. Blackstone represented the English constitution and common-law jurisdiction as solutions, tested by time and custom, to the problems of social conflict and the needs of orderly government. It is the persistence of these institutions over time and their inscription in the hearts of the English people that have created the love of liberty and the instinctive rejection of tyrannical government that are the true marks of English patriotism. This love of liberty is more the creation of custom and tradition than the expression of some spontaneous choice; and it is the long-term perspective of the common law that is the true fount of political order, rather than any contract between the citizens.

Blackstone's ideas have been influential throughout the subsequent centuries, and his defence of the common law has been taken up and amplified in our time by Friedrich von Hayek (see Chapter 5, below). He set the tone of Anglophone conservatism as it emerged through the eighteenth and nineteenth centuries: sceptical, empirical, focused on the concrete inheritance of a people and its institutions rather than on abstract ideas of political legitimacy designed to apply to all people everywhere. At the same time, he gave historical and empirical content to the theory of natural law by bringing it down from the theological stratosphere into the common-law courts of England, of which he was Lord Chief Justice.

Hobbes and Harrington wrote during a century of civil conflict, in which opinion was radically divided between the Parliamentary and Royalist factions. It was during the course of this conflict that the term 'Tory' was invented, to denote the traditionalist and loyalist sentiments that animated the Royalist factions in government. (The term comes from Irish *tóraighe*, a pursuer, used at the time to denote the dispossessed Irish who were attacking and molesting the English settlers.) Following the Glorious Revolution of 1688 the term entered general use to denote politicians and thinkers who were attached to the established customs and institutions of England – the monarchy and the Anglican Church especially – and who saw legitimacy as given by inheritance rather than created by choice.

Toryism was not so much a philosophy as a political practice, which pitted tradition and loyalty to the crown against the advocacy of liberal reforms. These reforms were calculated to capture power from the monarchy and distribute it to the modernising aristocracy – the 'Whig' faction in Parliament. (The term comes from Scots 'whiggamor' meaning a cattle driver, and used derisively by the Whigs' opponents, as the term 'Tory' had been used derisively by the Whigs.) The Glorious Revolution led to a century-long Whig ascendancy, though it was only with the formation of political parties in the nineteenth century – with the Tories becoming the Conservative Party and the Whigs the Liberals – that there was a hard and fast ideological division between the Parliamentary factions. (Thus the greatest of British conservative thinkers, Edmund Burke, was a Parliamentary Whig.)

Exactly why British politics settled, during the eighteenth century, around the Whig–Tory divide, and how that divide was connected to the religious and social conflicts that gave rise to it in the previous century, is a large historical question that is beyond the scope of this book. Suffice it to say that the term 'Tory', at first used to denounce those of Catholic and Stuart sympathies, was, during the course of the eighteenth century, domesticated, so as to apply to anyone for whom loyalty to the crown was more important than protests that might disturb the civil order. In this sense the term was used also at the time of the American Revolution, to describe those colonists who advocated loyalty to the king against the 'rebels' who supported American independence.

The beginnings of British intellectual conservatism are to be found in the works of educated writers who belonged, explicitly or implicitly, to the Tory camp. The two most interesting from our point of view were the Scottish philosopher David Hume (1711–76) and the English critic and poet Samuel Johnson (1709–84), and it is fitting to close this preliminary chapter with a brief summary of their views. Neither thinker dissented from the emerging individualist philosophy, and both regarded liberty as the foundation and the goal of civilised order. But neither believed in the liberal idea of the social contract or in the extravagant claims made by the followers of their contemporary Jean-Jacques Rousseau on behalf of the state of nature and the 'noble savage' who supposedly inhabited it.

Hume described himself as a Tory, not meaning to imply, however, that he subscribed either to the doctrine of the Anglican Church or to the divine right of the English kings, who by then were not English at all. He was almost certainly an atheist and believed in the established church and the established monarchy precisely because they were *established*, embodying in their structure and history the solutions to social conflicts and the tacit instructions for carrying on.

Hume's political philosophy is contained in his posthumously collected essays and in his six-volume *History of England* (1744) and is more fragmentary than the empiricist theory of knowledge for which he is nowadays more famous. He attacked the theory of the social contract, arguing that Locke's idea that we 'tacitly consent' to the government by voluntarily staying within its jurisdiction is a myth, most people being inevitably constrained by cultural, linguistic and habitual ties to stay where they are, whatever the government that legislates for them. Although he recognised the importance of popular consent in securing political order, he believed that consent is a *response* to the belief in legitimacy, rather than the foundation of it. The only true basis for any conception of legitimacy or political obligation, he argued, is utility, there being no other justification for obligations than the benefits that come from accepting them.

Hume believed that politics, as a 'moral' science, could be deduced from the study of human nature, and that controversies would dissolve if the true structure of our sentiments could be discerned. The principal sentiments involved in creating political order he identified as sympathy and benevolence, and he regarded the idea of justice as ultimately derived from them. Already we see in Hume a reaction to the Enlightenment project, of founding our political obligations in the exercise of reason. In all things that matter, and in particular all things on which our social being depends, it is custom not reason that provides the decisive motive.

Justice, Hume thought, required the establishment and defence of private rights, principal among which is the right of private property, for which he gave a classic utilitarian justification. He defended staunchly the liberties that he associated with the British constitution as this had emerged from the 'Glorious Revolution' and its aftermath, although he was extremely doubtful that those liberties could be easily guaranteed or that a formula could be found wherein to summarise them. His own preference was for a form of mixed republican and monarchical government, such as he argued was exhibited in Great Britain, where the two kinds of power oppose and limit each other.

The unsystematic nature of Hume's political ideas reflects his empiricist philosophy. Sceptical of abstract argument, and persuaded of the limitations of human knowledge, he pointed always to the utility of custom in guiding us along the path of peaceful coexistence. Grand liberal conceptions, in which the freedom of the individual is exalted into an absolute value to which all long-standing compromises must be sacrificed, were, he believed, to be distrusted. Such abstract conceptions were merely the latest of the enthusiasms that sweep from time to time across human societies, leaving death and destruction in their wake. The lesson of history for Hume is that established order, founded on customs that are followed and accepted, is always to be preferred to the ideas, however exultant and inspiring, of those who would liberate us from our inherited sense of obligation. This thought – the essence of Toryism throughout the modern era – is one to which Hume gave no further backing. But it was to become pivotal in the aftermath of the

French Revolution, when Burke set out to provide it with a philosophy.

Meanwhile, the reality of Toryism, as an *attitude* rather than a philosophy, was exemplified for all time by Hume's contemporary, Samuel Johnson. Dr Johnson, as he is known on account of the honorary doctorate conferred on him by the University of Oxford (in recognition of his great *Dictionary of the English Language*, 1755), was not a political philosopher, and did not engage in the kinds of argument about liberty and institutions that we find in Harrington and Locke. Yet he was and remains a towering intellectual presence in British national culture, an example of the rooted loyalty to 'things by law established' that has been, among so many Anglophone conservatives, their substitute for abstract argument. What Johnson believed he also exemplified, which was a firm moral sense combined with a robust eccentricity of manner and a deep respect for aesthetic values. For Johnson, the established church, which brought people together in a shared recognition of God's presence in their daily lives, was the heart of political order. Tolerance should be extended to dissenters and unbelievers, but not at the expense of orthodoxy. Poetry too was essential to political life as Johnson understood it, and here again the goal, for Johnson, was orthodoxy – the exact expression of moral truths, and the shaping of the language so that these truths could be understood and acted upon by all who share the literary culture.

Johnson's eccentric habits, amplified by what was probably Tourette's syndrome, and engagingly described by James Boswell in the *Life of Samuel Johnson* (1791), made his defence of orthodoxy all the more impressive. The search for the right opinion, the correct response, the sensible emotion was also, in Johnson's world, an expression of the highest freedom. He could be haughty and compassionate, indignant and remorseful by turns, but in everything he responded to the world with an exalted sense of responsibility for his own existence. Freedom, for Johnson, was not an escape from obligations, but a call to obey them, whether or not they have been consciously chosen. That was the Tory attitude, valuing eccentricity and independence as a sign of a deeper obedience than any sheepish conformity, and it has remained at the heart of English conservatism to this day.

The thinkers whose work I have touched on in this chapter belong to the pre-history of modern conservatism, to that moment when liberals and conservatives began to divide between them the new territory of post-religious politics. As I have argued, liberals and conservatives were united in their acceptance of individual liberty as an ultimate political value, but differed in their view of traditional institutions. Liberals saw political order as issuing from individual liberty; conservatives saw individual liberty as issuing from political order. What makes a political order legitimate, in the conservative view, is not the free choices that create it, but the free choices that it creates. The question of which comes first, liberty or order, was to divide liberals from conservatives for the next two hundred years. But in due course new threats came to unite them, not the least of them being the growth of the modern state.

# 2

# THE BIRTH OF PHILOSOPHICAL CONSERVATISM

As we have seen, conservatism began life more as a hesitation within liberalism than as a doctrine and philosophy in its own right. During the course of the eighteenth century, as the call for popular sovereignty gained momentum, leading first to the American Revolution and then to the French, the conservative hesitations began to crystallise as theories and policies. The difference in inspiration, trajectory and result between the American and the French revolutions is sometimes put down to the greater influence, in the American case, of conservative ways of thinking, compared with the romantic individualism, the desire to pull down the old order and to make everything anew, that inspired the revolutionaries in France. And the major influence here was Thomas Jefferson (1743–1826), who drafted the Declaration of Independence in 1776, and expounded, in his *Notes on the State of Virginia* (1784), a theoretical basis for what was to be the United States Constitution of 1788.

Jefferson was a conservative in the manner of Blackstone who saw American independence as ensuring the continuity of legal order against the lawless conduct of the English Crown. The Virginia Declaration of Rights (1776), drafted by Jefferson's friend George Mason, contained a résumé of rights extracted from and continuous with the common law, and Jefferson's subsequent observation of the French Revolution convinced him that, although there are universally valid human rights, the form of government must be tailored to the conditions of a given society, and not dictated by the logic of abstract ideas. Hence the common law would always be a better guide to defining rights than philosophical arguments. Jefferson also believed that generations, as well as individuals, have rights, and that a constitution should not be immovably imposed on future generations. The eventual adoption of a Bill of Rights as an amendment to the US Constitution owes much to his influence.

Jefferson is important in the history of conservatism for his insistence on continuity and custom as necessary conditions for successful constitution building, and also for his warnings against the centralisation of political power. He believed that the states of the Union should retain the powers necessary for local government and that the Federal powers of the Union should be the minimum required for its maintenance as a sovereign entity. Although guided by classical liberal philosophy – and notably by Locke, Harrington and Montesquieu – Jefferson believed social membership to be a part of liberty. He wished for an America of homesteads and settled communities, in which agrarian values would be properly respected and towns and institutions built according to civilised principles. In his own estate at Monticello and in the University of Virginia that he established in Charlottesville Jefferson set an example of conservatism in action – adopting classical architecture and a traditional curriculum that would emphasise the continuity of the new country with the old order of Europe. Although the constitution that he helped to draft was democratic in form, Jefferson believed that it stood in need of those customs that give a voice to past generations, and he saw these customs as part of our attachment to the soil.

True, the agrarian way of life that Jefferson advocated was infected at the time with a serious moral flaw – the slavery that he did not defend in his writings, but nevertheless exploited in his life. However, his emphasis on the land, and the art of settling it, was to form a dominant theme in American conservatism throughout the two centuries that followed.

This has marked a growing division between American 'classical' liberals and their conservative opponents. The heirs to the liberals soon moved towards a political vision focused on market economics, manufacture and free trade; they saw cities not as settlements but as centres of production and exchange; and the values of efficiency, mobility and economic growth quickly rose to the top of their agenda. In the contemporary situation, if they have taken note of farming it is as a kind of business – agribusiness – which must follow the way of all trade and get bigger in order to survive. In this way the 'free market' tendency of American politics has led to the destruction of the landscape. The conservatives, by contrast, have on the whole been moved by a vision of settled communities, united as 'one nation under God', attached to the land and the family, and building their cities as centres of civilisation. Their ideal America is typified by beautiful settlements like Charleston and the old New York and Boston of Henry James. Thanks to the liberal tendency, which places utilitarian above aesthetic values, those great cities, like the landscape, are now being uglified to extinction. Nevertheless, the divide remains in American conservative politics between the Jeffersonian defence of an agrarian civilisation, and the championing of market forces against the collectivist state. (See Chapter 5, below.)

In this connection we should note the importance of *The Federalist* Papers, a series of eighty-five articles by Alexander Hamilton, James Madison and John Jay, published under the pseudonym of Publius, in support of the campaign for the ratification of the US Constitution in 1787–8. Wide-ranging and eminently practical in tone, the Papers attempt to apply the pure liberal doctrines garnered from Locke, Harrington, Montesquieu and others, to the emerging condition of America, as a would-be federation of separately constituted States. While *The Federalist* Papers are now understood as one of the leading statements of the liberal position, they have also been an important input into American conservatism, raising the question of the constitutional safeguards of individual liberty against the growth of a centralised government, and providing the ground for conservative campaigns on behalf of 'States' rights'.

The American Founders were serious people, educated in political and constitutional thinking, who created one of the most important documents in modern history – the first real attempt to provide a constitution that both specified the powers of government, and also insisted that those were the *only* powers, adding a Bill of Rights, in due course, to emphasise the point. Exactly what this document means today is a question to which I return in Chapter

6. But, whatever the weight of philosophy behind it, the Constitution is a legal and not a philosophical statement, and leaves the philosophical arguments roughly where they were in the aftermath of Locke.

The Enlightenment saw the birth of the social sciences, with rival schools of economists – 'mercantilist' and 'physio-crat' – emerging in France, which country also saw the publication of comparative studies of the religions and social organisations of indigenous peoples. Much of the new sociological approach to human communities entered the *Encyclopédie* of d'Alembert and Diderot (1751–72), the great work of Enlightenment scepticism which had religion, tradition and aristocracy as its target, and which helped to prepare the way for the French Revolution. But it was a thinker of the Scottish Enlightenment, Adam Smith (1723–90), who provided the philosophical insight that gave intellectual conservatism its first real start in life.

Smith published little and destroyed most of his manuscripts before his death. But his two major published works – *The Theory of Moral Sentiments* (1759) and *The Wealth of Nations* (1776), together with his surviving *Lectures on Jurisprudence* (1762–6) – express a vision of civil society which has since become central to the conservative position, both in the Anglophone world and elsewhere. *The Theory of Moral Sentiments* sees the foundation of human communities in our disposition to seek a 'mutual sympathy of sentiments', as we strive to unite with others in our approval or disapproval of each other's acts. We are conscious of ourselves not only as agents, animated by our own desires, but also as objects of judgement in the eyes of others. Hence we inevitably see ourselves from outside, as others see us, and seek for their approval and sympathy, which is the greatest of social goods. Thus arises in human communities the habit of consulting, in imagination, the 'impartial spectator', in order to assess our own thoughts, feelings and actions and to reach a verdict as to their moral worth.

Smith developed this theory with many fine observations of social emotions, analysing conscience, remorse, blame and admiration, and recognising the sense of accountability to the other as the core of the moral life. Although Smith does not explicitly address the political question of how liberty is secured, his argument brings to the fore the truth (which his friend David Hume also took to be the foundation of moral philosophy) that a society of free individuals is founded in sympathetic feelings, not in reason.

Smith saw justice as a negative virtue, which consists in the disposition to refrain from injuring others or from taking what is rightfully theirs. This virtue is the essential foundation of a well-ordered society, but the sentiment for it is too feeble to be effective without the support of law. In the *Lectures on Jurisprudence* Smith develops this idea, arguing that common-law rights are an exposition of the negative idea of justice. These rights are paid for by our legal duties, and the principal purpose of the court of law is to assign responsibility for our actions, so as to determine who should be judged and how.

The picture of civil society that Smith paints is one that has become fundamental to the conservative vision in our time. Civil society is, indeed, composed of individuals, acting freely: this much Smith accepts. But freedom entails responsibility, founded in the sentiments of sympathy that make us strive to look on our own and others' conduct from the standpoint of the impartial judge. The institutions of law and government exist in order to assign responsibilities and to ensure that they are not evaded or abused. Of course, this is something that liberals too will acknowledge. But the difference of emphasis is crucial to the conservative position. Conservatism is about freedom, yes. But it is also about the institutions and attitudes that shape the responsible citizen, and ensure that freedom is a benefit to us all. Conservatism is therefore also about the limits to freedom. And here, in the potential conflict with the extreme liberal view that values freedom above all other things and refuses to set limits to its exercise, we encounter one of the principal political issues of our time.

Although *The Theory of Moral Sentiments* was esteemed by Smith as his most important work, and although he was constantly adding to and amending it throughout his life, he is more famous now for his *Inquiry into the Nature and Causes of the Wealth of Nations*, the book that gave the first serious defence of the market economy from philosophical principles. Smith opposed the mercantilist belief that a state's power depends upon its wealth, and that the best policy for a state is to retain as much wealth within its borders as possible. That static vision of wealth, as an accumulation of stuff, misrepresents the true nature of economic value, which depends on the circulation of goods through trade, and on the investment and use of human labour.

Smith was the first thinker to see the efficient use of labour as the fount of economic development. The division of labour, which enables people to devote their talents to one item of production, and to exchange the surplus for the other things that they need, is, for Smith, the true cause of economic progress. But he also recognised that the 'detail division' of labour within the manufacturing process threatened to reduce the labourer to a mechanical shadow, and he foresaw in this the breakdown of social order that would follow, if the effects of the Industrial Revolution were not mitigated by laws protecting the social well-being of the workforce.

Smith believed that a market economy, while not without its evils, has a natural tendency to equilibrium. In a market, 'every individual is continually exerting himself to find out the most advantageous employment for whatever capital he can command.' Through intending his own gain, a merchant, labourer or owner of capital contributes to the general welfare, 'led by an invisible hand to promote an end which was no part of his intention'. Critics point out that the market system may produce vast inequalities, and that this may in itself destroy the possibility of equilibrium in the political sphere. But the core of the argument is untouched by that criticism. It lies in the 'invisible hand' conception of human society, and in the idea that collective solutions may be most effective when not directly intended. This argument has proven to be, in the long run, crucial to the philosophy of conservatism.

The argument tells us that, in conditions of normal social interaction, self-interested individuals, acting freely, will promote outcomes that benefit them all. They do not *intend* these outcomes, still less do they plan them. The outcomes are the unintended by-product of decisions that make no reference to them. Invisible-hand effects are not observed only in the economic sphere. The beauty of traditional villages built with local materials is the unintended by-product of the desire for durable shelter at the lowest cost. Peace between nations is the unintended by-product of trade between their citizens. And so on, for other unintended but repeatable consequences, both good and bad. But the point of Smith's argument is deeper than that suggests. For him the invisible-hand mechanism is not just an explanation of the market: it is a *justification* too. It is precisely because the price (or 'exchange value') of goods in a market issues from the free transactions of individuals that it is a sure guide to trade. It is a distillation of social knowledge, which enables each participant in the market to respond to the desires and needs of every other.

Moreover, the argument suggests that those who plan the production and distribution of goods in a great society are trying to achieve the impossible. The plan is bound to interfere with the free relations between people, and thereby to destroy the normal and unintended effects of human freedom, economic coordination being one of them. Planning, in such circumstances, threatens to destroy the human relations on which it depends.

The argument, developed at length by economists of the Austrian school (see Chapter 5), has been pivotal in modern revivals of the conservative message. For it suggests that it is not the state but civil society – the free associations between individuals – that contains the solution to pressing collective problems, and therefore that it is not state control but individual liberty that is needed by a great society for its success.

The objection is made that market solutions are not always available, and that, left to itself, the market may erode the conditions on which it depends, by encouraging the predators, the cheats, the monopolists and those who would put everything, human relations included, up for sale. But this is not an argument for rejecting Smith's 'invisible hand'. Rather it is an argument for recognising the truth that he was trying to put across in *The Theory of Moral Sentiments* – namely that, in normal conditions, people respond sympathetically to each other's actions, hold themselves accountable, and seek the favourable judgement that they also wish to bestow. A market economy presupposes honest people who wish to reach deals openly and by agreement. Hence it must always be backed up by the moral and legal strictures that issue from our shared fund of sympathy, and will not otherwise be secure against the frauds, the abusers and the cheats.

All this becomes clearer when we turn to the other great eighteenth-century British conservative, the incomparable Edmund Burke, whose career as a parliamentarian and statesman gave added authority to the essays and pamphlets through which he attempted to develop a full response to the challenge of popular sovereignty, and in particular to its pathological manifestation, as he saw it, in the French Revolution. The American Revolution, which ended in 1783, led to the Philadelphia Convention of 1787, in which the former colonists drew up the liberal constitution that has served to govern the United States ever since.

The French Revolution of 1789 set out at first to emulate the American, with the newly formed Assemblée Nationale issuing a 'Declaration of the Rights of Man and of the Citizen', which was impeccable in its advocacy of liberal freedoms. The document, drafted by Jefferson's friend the Marquis de Lafayette, who had played an important part in the American Revolution, was intended to provide the same foundation to the new political order as had been provided by the US Constitution.

However, there were significant differences between the two documents. The American Constitution, and the Bill of Rights that was added to it under the influence of James Madison and Jefferson, were indelibly marked by common-law jurisdiction, and understood by all signatories as an attempt to protect the ancient rights and privileges of the people, as defined and discovered by the law. In other words, the US Constitution was designed to guarantee to the people what they had once enjoyed, before the Crown began to tax them without authority. It was the residue of an already established practice rather than a recipe for a new order of things.

The French Declaration was the product of philosophical reflection, an attempt to transcribe into politics ideas that had previously had no overt presence there, and which owed as much to the abstract arguments of philosophers as to the American example. In particular it made no reference to the institutions of government, and defined the rights of man and the citizen without reference to any procedure that might be used to uphold them in a court of law. It was a work of philosophy, imbued with the a priori spirit of Rousseau, whose theory of the 'general will' is explicitly invoked in Article VI, and for whom human beings and their imperfections had always been an impediment to his ideal of an uncorrupted order of freedom. Moreover, the Assembly, in issuing the Declaration, made a distinction between 'active' and 'passive' citizens, the former being the minority that was expressly protected by the Declaration, the latter being the vast majority (women, peasants, servants and the propertyless classes) who would be protected only indirectly, by those active citizens who had charge of them.

No writer perceived the defects of the Declaration as clearly as Edmund Burke, whose commentary on the French Revolution, *Reflections on the Recent Revolution in France* (1790), written in the year after the Revolution had been set in motion, is an astonishing example of his ability to see to the heart of things and to predict the way in which they are bound to go. Although, when Burke wrote, the king had not been executed, and the Terror had not begun, he foresaw both those events, and warned against what he saw as the principal defect of the French Revolution, when compared with the American (which he had defended), namely that it was imposed on the people from above, by a 'literary cabal'. And against this he developed a complex, unsystematic but highly illuminating account of custom, tradition and civil association in terms of which to diagnose the destructive nature of that kind of 'geometrical' (i.e. abstract and deductive) politics.

Burke here recognises that freedom is always in jeopardy and must be protected by the law. And he is clear that a modern society must be organised politically, by a government that is to a certain measure independent of religious, tribal and family ties. But he defends religion and family as forms of collective wisdom, while rejecting the extreme individualism that refuses to acknowledge the indispensable part played by social membership in the exercise of free rational choice. Burke's argument gives a detailed and subtle defence of the social inheritance that makes popular sovereignty possible, against the intellectuals who wish to tear down all settled laws and institutions in the people's name.

Burke rejected the liberal idea of the social contract, as a deal agreed among living people. Society, he argued, does not contain the living only; it is an association between the dead, the living and the unborn. Its binding principle is not contract but something more akin to trusteeship. It is a shared inheritance for the sake of which we learn to circumscribe our demands, to see our own place in things as part of a continuous chain of giving and receiving, and to recognise that the good things we inherit are not ours to spoil but ours to safeguard for our dependents. There is a line of obligation that connects us to those who gave us what we have; and our concern for the future is an extension of that line. We take the future of our community into account not by fictitious cost–benefit calculations, but more concretely, by seeing ourselves as inheriting benefits and passing them on. Concern for future generations is a non-specific outgrowth of gratitude. It does not calculate, because it shouldn't and can't.

Burke's complaint against the revolutionaries was that they assumed the right to spend all trusts and endowments on their own self-made emergency. Schools, church foundations, hospitals – all institutions that had been founded by people, now dead, for the benefit of their successors – were expropriated or destroyed, the result being the total waste of accumulated savings, leading to massive inflation, the collapse of education and the loss of the traditional forms of social and medical relief. In this way contempt for the dead leads to the disenfranchisement of the unborn, and although that result is not, perhaps, inevitable, it has been repeated by all subsequent revolutions. Through their contempt for the intentions and emotions of those who had laid things by, revolutions have systematically destroyed the stock of social capital, and always revolutionaries justify this by impeccable utilitarian reasoning. Radical individualists enter the world without social capital of their own, and they consume all that they find.

As important for Burke as the concept of trusteeship was that of the 'little platoon'. Society, he believed, depends upon relations of affection and trust, and these can be built only from below, through face-to-face interaction. It is in the family, in local clubs and societies, in school, church, team, regiment and university that people learn to interact as free beings, each taking responsibility for his actions and accounting to his neighbour. When society is organised from above, either by the top-down government of a revolutionary dictatorship, or by the impersonal edicts of an inscrutable bureaucracy, then accountability rapidly disappears from the political order, and from society too.

Top-down government breeds irresponsible individuals, and the confiscation of civil society by the state leads to a widespread refusal among the citizens to act for themselves. Against the society of conscripts initiated by the French revolutionaries Burke wished to propose a society of volunteers. And this meant that for Burke, as for all subsequent conservatives, civil society has been the true fount of social order and authority, rather than the state – a point that depended upon Hegel for its full philosophical elaboration. (See the next chapter.)

'Little platoons' are the places where traditions form. Social traditions, Burke pointed out, are forms of knowledge. They contain the residues of many trials and errors, and the inherited solutions to problems that we all encounter. Like those cognitive abilities that pre-date civilisation they are *adaptations*, but adaptations of the community rather than of the individual organism. Social traditions exist because they enable a society to reproduce itself. Destroy them heedlessly and you remove the guarantee offered by one generation to the next.

Burke's argument parallels the argument for the market economy hinted at by Adam Smith and given in full, 150 years later, by the Austrian economists. (See Chapter 5.) Only in a free market, argued Mises and Hayek, does the information exist that enables individual players to dispense their budget rationally. For only in a free market do prices provide a guide to the economic needs of others. Prices distil information about the indefinitely many strangers living now.[4] In a similar way, for Burke, traditions and customs distil information about the indefinitely many strangers

4   The argument that I have here condensed is spelled out in detail
    in Ludwig von Mises, *Socialism: An Economic and Sociological
    Analysis*, London, 1951 (first published 1922 as *Die Gemeinwirtschaft:
    Untersuchungen über den Sozialismus*), and in the essays in Hayek's
    *Individualism and Economic Order*, Chicago, 1948, especially the three
    essays on 'Socialist Calculation' there reprinted. See Chapter 5 below.

living *then*, information that we need if we are to accommodate our conduct to the needs of absent generations.

Moreover, in discussing tradition, we are not discussing arbitrary rules and conventions. We are discussing *answers* that have been discovered to enduring *questions*. These answers are tacit, shared, embodied in social practices and inarticulate expectations. Those who adopt them are not necessarily able to explain them, still less to justify them. Hence Burke described them as 'prejudices', and defended them on the grounds that, though the stock of reason in each individual is small, there is an accumulation of reason in society that we question and reject at our peril.

Reason therefore shows itself in that about which we do not, and maybe cannot, reason – and this is what we see in our traditions, including those traditions that contain sacrifice at the heart of them, such as military honour, family giving and the worship of the gods. Burke adds that 'prejudice, with its reason, has a motive to give action to that reason, and an affection that will give it permanence. Prejudice is of ready application in the emergency; it previously engages the mind in a steady course of wisdom and virtue, and does not leave the man hesitating in the moment of decision, sceptical, puzzled, and unresolved. Prejudice renders a man's virtue his habit; and not a series of unconnected acts. Through just prejudice, his duty becomes a part of his nature.'

In Burke's understanding, therefore, tradition is a form of *knowledge*. Not theoretical knowledge, of course, concerning facts and truths; and not ordinary know-how either. There is another kind of knowledge, which is neither knowledge *that* nor knowledge *how*, which involves the mastery of situations – knowing *what to do*, in order to accomplish a task successfully, where success is not measured in any exact or fore-envisaged goal, but in the harmony of the result with our human needs and interests. Good manners illustrate what Burke had in mind. Knowing what to do in company, what to say, what to feel – these are things we acquire by immersion in society. They cannot be taught by spelling them out but only by osmosis, yet the person who has not acquired these things is rightly described as ignorant. Moreover, they illustrate the way in which those higher forms of practical knowledge – Aristotle's virtues – are acquired and exercised, and the influence of Aristotle is apparent in the passage from Burke that I just quoted.

Although the social contract exists in many forms, its ruling principle was announced by Hobbes with the assertion that there can be 'no obligation on any man which ariseth not from some act of his own'.[5] My obligations are my own creation, binding because freely chosen. When you and I exchange promises, the resulting contract is freely undertaken, and any breach does violence not merely to the other but also to the self, since it is a repudiation of a well-grounded rational choice. If we could construe our obligation to the state on the model of a contract, therefore, we would have justified it in terms that all rational beings must accept. Contracts are the paradigms of self-chosen obligations – obligations that are not imposed, commanded or coerced but freely undertaken. When law is founded in a social contract, therefore, obedience to the law is simply the

5   Thomas Hobbes, *Leviathan*, part 2, ch. 21.

other side of free choice. Freedom and obedience are one and the same. That was the idea that Rousseau exalted into the ruling principle of politics. Law and legislation would be the expression of a 'general will', which, because it was the will of every citizen, would ensure that every act of obedience was also an expression of free choice.

Rousseau's social contract begins from an assembly of abstract individuals, who are without ties or attachments, and who have nothing to guide their social conduct other than the agreements that they can make with their fellows. This picture of society was shared too by the revolutionaries, for whom the old order was to be pulled down in its entirety, so that people could start again with nothing to guide them save their own free choice. But social beings are not like that, as Burke insisted. Societies are by their nature exclusive, establishing privileges and benefits that are offered only to the insider, and that cannot be freely bestowed on all comers without sacrificing the trust on which social harmony depends. The social contract begins from a thought experiment, in which a group of people gather together to decide on their common future. But if they are in a position to decide on their common future, it is because they already have one: because they recognise their mutual togetherness and reciprocal dependence, which makes it incumbent upon them to settle how they might be governed under a common jurisdiction in a common territory. In short, the social contract requires a relation of membership, and one, moreover, which makes it plausible for the individual members to conceive the relation between them in contractual terms. Theorists of the social contract write as though it presupposes only the first-person singular of free rational choice. In fact, it presupposes a first-person plural, in which the burdens of belonging have already been assumed.

The aim of Burke's argument in the *Reflections* is to uphold the priority of the 'we' over the 'I', and to warn against what happens when the forms of social membership are taken away and society disintegrates, as he put it, into the 'dust and powder of individuality'. The 'we' that he advocates is not that of the modern bureaucratic state, still less that of the revolutionary guardians who speak on behalf of the people while never consulting them. It is the 'we' of a traditional community, bound by the web of 'little platoons' under a shared rule of law and a territorial sovereignty. It is what we should now call a 'nation', though without the belligerent ideology of nationalism with which the French revolutionaries had bolstered their power.

Burke was explicitly contrasting the form of reasoning that emerges through custom, free exchange and 'prejudice' with the a priori principles of the revolutionaries, which they attributed to the abstract 'reason' that is supposedly everyone's inheritance. As already suggested, he upheld customs and traditions not merely because he saw them as the object of affection and trust but because he understood them as forms of social knowledge: the kind of knowledge that the rationalism of the revolutionaries was fated to destroy, and the destruction of which leads to the ever-increasing absolutism and exorbitance of those who are striving to govern without it.

Burke's argument was to be rephrased in other terms,

in Oakeshott's attack on 'rationalism in politics', in Hayek's defence of 'spontaneous order', and in T. S. Eliot's defence of tradition, and I shall therefore return to it. Its importance is rarely understood by its critics, who read the *Reflections* as a work of nostalgia, a belated attempt to defend a doomed society from the necessary modernisation that had been delayed for far too long. In fact Burke's argument was a diagnosis of what goes wrong when the relation between the free individual and the orderly community is misconstrued. The revolutionaries idolised individual liberty, and invoked it at every stage of their adventure. Even the Revolutionary Tribunals, in which judge, jury and prosecution were one and the same, and the accused was denied the right of defence, were justified by what Robespierre called 'the despotism of liberty'. But this liberty, construed as the foundation of social order, was indistinguishable from tyranny. And that was exactly what we should expect, since liberty is not the foundation of social order but one of its by-products. To borrow Adam Smith's idiom, liberty arises by an invisible hand from practices that do not intend it, but which embody the socially engendered knowledge of generations. Take away custom, tradition, and the little platoons and you take away the shield between the people and the one who seeks to control them, and who claims to be speaking in their name. Real popular sovereignty, Burke implies, involves respect for what the people themselves respect – namely tradition, law and the narrative of legitimate order.

Of all the reactions to the French Revolution, Burke's was surely the most eloquent and damning. But it was presented without any claim to philosophical system, and was savagely attacked by those radicals for whom the rights of the individual are the sole source of political legitimacy, one of whom, Thomas Paine, was to play an active part, first in French and then in American politics, as a champion of the people against the establishment (*Rights of Man*, 1791 2). The original declaration of 'The Rights of Man and of the Citizen' was to be followed by a statement of the duties of man and of the citizen, but the Assemblée Nationale concluded that such a statement was unnecessary. It therefore moved quickly from orderly government to the moral vacuum that arises when a society is based entirely on claims against it rather than duties towards it. Looking back on the conflict from our position today we can surely recognise, in the writings of Smith and Burke, an attempt to describe the sentiment of social membership in terms that put duty and responsibility where they belong, at the heart of the social order. But it is the shallow arguments of Thomas Paine that have had the greatest influence, illustrating the burden under which conservatives have always laboured, which is that of defending a position that is rich in demands, but poor in promises.

# 3

# CONSERVATISM IN GERMANY AND FRANCE

The first two chapters of this book have shown conservative ideas arising in the English-speaking world in tandem with a liberal conception of political order. Seeking to mount a case for popular sovereignty, liberals encounter certain inconvenient realities. Human beings, they discover, are freely choosing individuals, but only when set in the social context that makes them so. Freedom is a human good, certainly, but only when limited in ways that prevent its abuse. Liberal laws are the triumph of political order, but only when the people have the social knowledge required to understand and obey them. And in response to those realities the conservative steps in with an alternative philosophy. Only where customs and traditions exist will the sovereignty of the individual lead to true political order rather than to anarchy; only in a community of non-contractual obligations will society have the stability and moral order that make secular government possible.

The relation between liberalism and conservatism, as I have described it, therefore, is not one of absolute antagonism, but rather one of symbiosis. Liberalism makes sense only in the social context that conservatism defends. But liberals and conservatives are temperamentally quite distinct. Liberals naturally rebel, conservatives naturally obey.

Destroy the culture of obedience, conservatives believe, so that rights are declared but duties forgotten, and the result is the totalitarian terror that followed the French Revolution.

The same dialectical relation between liberalism and conservatism was played out elsewhere, and most memorably in the political writings of two great German philosophers, Immanuel Kant (1724–1804) and Georg Wilhelm Friedrich Hegel (1770–1831). Kant was a liberal, and on one interpretation an extreme one, since he made the freely choosing individual into the very centre of his world view, and judged all institutions and procedures in terms of that one idea. He argued that morality, law and politics, correctly understood, issue from 'autonomy of the will'. However, this autonomy is expressed through duty, not desire. The free being is constrained by reason to accept the categorical imperative, which applies to all rational beings and which tells us that we should act according to that maxim which we could also at the same time will to be a universal law, treating all persons equally as 'ends in themselves'.

Despite this emphasis on duty, Kant's moral and political philosophy makes no special place for customs and traditions; it takes no real account of family or the 'little platoon', and it attempts to spell out the realm of rights and duties from an abstract and a priori theory that makes no reference to any specific historical community. Kant drew radical political conclusions of a kind that coincided, by and large, with the emerging liberal orthodoxies, though always with the emphasis on duties and law, rather than rights and liberation. He was an admirer of Rousseau, and a defender (at least initially) of the French Revolution. He expounded a version of the social contract theory, while arguing for a 'cosmopolitan' world order, in which nation states would coexist with diminished sovereignty under international law. And he advocated republican government, administered by the elected representatives of the people.

Hegel saw Kant's philosophy as a defence of 'abstract right' – the web of rights and duties defined by reason alone, and without reference to the history or particularity of human relations. For Hegel, this abstract right, although valid in itself, must also become concrete, united with the historical attachments of real moral agents, if it is to issue in definite guidance. Without the concrete demands of the moral order the idea of right remains in the intellectual stratosphere, failing to come to earth in any real application. From the confrontation between abstract right and concrete morality the sphere of ethical life emerges.

Political order is the communal expression of this ethical life (*Sittlichkeit*), and Hegel's defence of it is a highly original and metaphysically intriguing version of the conservative response to liberalism. Hegel set out to show that the abstract freedom of Kant and Rousseau is only available in the context of a tradition-governed social order, in which non-contractual obligations and corporate institutions form the web of social membership. In the transition from Kant to Hegel we discover a metaphysical version of the transition that we have already examined, in considering the views of Locke and Burke: the transition from liberal aspirations to conservative realities.

Hegel was profoundly influenced by Kant. But he was influenced just as much by the aftermath of the eighteenth-century revolutions. Those revolutions irreversibly changed the image of politics. Henceforth political thought was to be infected by the idea that everything can be changed utterly, that institutions and laws are no more than temporary measures, and that the onus is on those who defend the status quo to find a reason for conserving it, and a reason sufficient to override all the hopes and dreams of the radicals. Soon theories emerged to explain, justify and advocate revolution, and one of them, that of Marx, has dominated political thought and practice ever since.

Marx's vision owes everything to Hegel, whose principal conceptions Marx adopted, adapted and travestied in his attempt to seize the high ground of political advocacy. Like his 'Young Hegelian' followers, of whom Marx was one, Hegel accepted the French Revolution as a profound turning point, and a coming to consciousness of the deep undercurrents of history. In this and in other ways it is possible to represent Hegel as a founder of nineteenth-century revolutionary politics. Nevertheless, despite his initial admiration for Napoleon, and his life-long addiction to the Hero as a redemptive figure, Hegel's political philosophy evolved into the most systematic presentation that we have of the conservative vision of political order.

The starting point of conservative philosophy is admirably captured by Hegel in *The Phenomenology of Spirit* (1806), which shows how relations of conflict and domination are overcome by the recognition of mutual rights and duties, and how, in the course of this, individuals achieve not only freedom of action, but also a sense of their social membership. The process whereby human beings acquire their freedom, Hegel shows, also builds their attachments. The institutions of law, education and politics are part of this – not things that we freely choose from a position of detachment, but things through which we acquire our freedom, and without which we could not exist as fully self-conscious agents.

The freely choosing self of Rousseau is, for Hegel, an empty abstraction. The self does not exist prior to society, but is created in society, through the resolution of conflict, and through custom, morality and civil association. These constitute the immovable 'given' of the human condition, for without them there cannot be the self-conscious aware-ness on which our world is founded. Hegel argues for this conclusion in a remarkable way, by considering the para-doxical nature of slavery (*Phenomenology of Spirit*, chapter 4, part 1).

Hegel presents our social evolution in a series of scen-arios, showing the development from undifferentiated species life to the self-conscious individuality of the polit-ical animal. He writes of a transition from the 'life and death' struggle in the state of nature to relations of domination, when the 'I' emerges in conflict with the 'you'. The conflict is resolved by victory, when one or the other gives way, pre-ferring slavery to death: 'I' now dominates 'you'. As master I have the power to command your labour. But it is you, the slave, who imprint your mark on the world, since you are maker and creator of the products on which I depend. I, as consumer, find nothing of myself in the world that I enjoy: all is dimmed by my indolence, and even the belief in my freedom suffers, since I have effectively surrendered my will to the other who works for me. True freedom involves consciousness of my autonomy, and this I can acquire only if others recognise it, in free and equal dealings. I might try to command this recognition from you: but recognition that is commanded is not the recognition that I seek, which must be freely bestowed, if it is to confirm my right to it.

In this way, Hegel suggests, power relations are imbued with a kind of contradiction. The master seeks recognition from the slave, who has no power to bestow it. Only by relinquishing his domination can the master enjoy true autonomy as a free agent. Hegel's 'dialectic' – the process whereby contradictions are first generated and then resolved – implies that the contradiction in the heart of the master–slave relationship will be transcended. Mutual recognition will replace domination. Each now will have the whole of freedom: the power to exercise it and the recognition that makes it worthwhile. Thus Hegel argues that true freedom necessitates obedience to the 'abstract right' of Kant, and in particular to the law that enjoins us to respect all persons not as means only but as ends in themselves. Only this will resolve the contradictions in which we are otherwise bound by our attempts to escape from the state of nature.

Many thoughts are suggested by the parable of the master and the slave, and conservatives have no monopoly over its interpretation. (The outlines of Hegel's argument survived in Marx's theories throughout their many evolving versions.) But for the conservative, the argument is important as a challenge to the fundamental metaphysics of liberal individualism. If Hegel is right then freedom is a social artefact, born out of conflict, submission and struggle.

Moreover the 'equality of respect' which liberals and socialists both esteem as the foundation of civilised order comes
into existence inherently tainted by conflict. Such equality
is to be won out of inequality, and the ideal of an absolute
equality, free from the marks of power and domination, is
no more than a delusion. The history of freedom survives in
the very nature of freedom, and it is a history of bondage.
The freedom that Hegel ascribes to us is therefore both
political and profoundly anti-utopian.

The *Phenomenology of Spirit* was Hegel's first mature
work and the key to all his subsequent reflections. But it
does not attempt to spell out a political message in any
detail. Instead it reflects on the various stages through
which consciousness is 'determined' and 'realised' in the life
of the individual. It is an incomparable account of the complexity of the inner life, represented as a series of 'dialectical'
transitions – successive contradictions and their resolu-
tions – in the progress of the spirit towards full consciousness of itself. In *Outlines of the Philosophy of Right* (1821),
Hegel applies the same dialectical vision to political order,
in which freedom is realised as a collective state of being.

Politics, for Hegel, is an elaboration of *Sittlichkeit*, 'ethical
life', which is the public and outward aspect of morality. The
structure of the dialectic is manifested in the tension and
conflict between two forms of association – the family and
civil society (*bürgerliche Gesellschaft*) – and the resolution
of this conflict in the state, which is the highest of institutions. Like Burke, Hegel saw the family as a key element in
political order, the sphere of the attachments from which
the individual first sets out on the journey to freedom and

self-knowledge. It is also the source of unchosen obligations, which surround individuals at birth, invading their
freedom even before they have truly acquired it. Such obligations belong to the household (and are symbolised for
Hegel in the Roman household gods, or *penates*). Disloyalty
to the household is a form of disloyalty to the self, since it
involves the rejection of the conditions from which will and
reason first emerge. Hence it is an essential part of freedom
to recognise obligations that are not freely chosen (obligations of piety). All the arguments for thinking that rational
beings must (as the liberal supposes) recognise the legitimacy of contracts are therefore also arguments for saying
that they must recognise legitimacy in something else. It is
this something else – the sphere of non-contractual obligations – that the conservative philosopher must describe and
the conservative politician uphold.

Thus marriage, which begins in a contract, cannot be
understood as a contractual obligation. Rather it is a 'sub-
stantial tie', and the life involved in it is 'life in its totality
– i.e. as the actuality of the race, and its life-process'. This
union, which is a self-restriction, is also a liberation, since
it endows the parties to it with a new consciousness of the
validity of their common world. Such relationships are naturally endowed with a consecrated quality by those who are
party to them, and the sense of political obligation can be
seen as a recuperation at the highest level of the sense of the
sacred that is first acquired through the ties of family life.

Civil society is the sphere of free association and of
institutions that arise by an 'invisible hand' (by what Hegel
calls 'the cunning of reason'). It is the arena of spontaneous

membership, in which we group together in the 'little platoons' of Burke, in shared enterprises, churches, clubs and corporations. Hegel was strongly influenced by the Roman-law concept of the corporate person, as an entity possessing rights and duties of its own. As corporations, he believed, the spontaneous associations of civil society acquire a moral identity. Such associations are rooted in private property, through which we express our trust and affection in gift and free exchange. For Hegel, private property is also the natural expression and realisation (the *Entäusserung* or 'externalisation') of individual freedom in the world of objects.

Just as marriage is not a contract but an existential tie, so is it 'equally far from the truth to ground the nature of the state on a contractual relation ... the intrusion of this contractual relation, and of relationships concerning private property in general, into the relation between the individual and the state, has been productive of the greatest confusion in both constitutional law and public life'. Like Burke, Hegel saw the idea of a social contract as introducing an illusion of choice where there is no choice, leading us to treat in instrumental terms an arrangement – legal sovereignty – which can be properly understood only as an end in itself.

Hegel does not dismiss Rousseau's vision entirely. For he agrees with Rousseau that the state is a person: it has agency, will and identity through time. It forms plans, entertains reasons – which may be good or bad – and takes responsibility for its actions. (Such at least is the state in its true or actualised form.) This personal state is 'the actuality of the ethical idea'. Its rights and duties transcend those of the individual and like any person it must be treated not as a means only but as an end in itself: its survival is non-negotiable.

It is because the state has this identity as an ethical person that it must be distinguished from civil society. Associated with the social contract theory is the equally unacceptable idea that civil society and the state are one and the same, which would imply that membership of the state is something optional. Only if we clearly distinguish the state from the totality of civil associations will we understand political obligation, which is not a contractual deal, like a business partnership, but a binding tie, comparable in this matter to the non-contractual tie to the family.

Perhaps the most significant development in modern politics has been the emergence of political systems with the opposite vice to that criticised by Hegel: the vice not of dissolving the state in civil society but of absorbing civil society into the state. This vice was exhibited already by the Jacobins, who effectively outlawed all associations that they did not control, and was the conscious policy of the Communists in the Soviet Union and its empire. The autonomous institutions (Hegel's 'corporations') – which are the core of civil society – were all subverted, and no association was permitted which was not under the control of the Party, which also controlled the state. The history of totalitarianism aptly vindicates the two major conceptions of Hegel's political philosophy: the theory that state and civil society can flourish only when not confounded, and the theory that the state, in its proper form, has the identity and authority of a corporate person. Precisely by using the state to suppress all corporations and autonomous associations, the totalitarians established an impersonal and unaccountable machine in the place of responsible government. Destroying the freedom of the citizens, including the freedom to associate, they also destroyed the personality of the state, which became a kind of mask worn by the conspiratorial Party.

The importance of the distinction between state and civil society is not always recognised, and was obscured by the eighteenth-century habit of using the term 'civil society' to denote every kind of political order. Hegel was perhaps the first conservative fully to appreciate that the state introduces a new order of agency, one that cannot be reduced to, or constructed from, the powers of civil associations. Hence the freedom of the citizen that is guaranteed by the state, is also threatened by the state. The state can uphold liberty only if it withdraws from civil society, which means that civil society must have a self-sustaining order of its own – the order associated with Smith's 'invisible hand', Burke's 'prejudice', and Hegel's 'cunning of reason'.

As well as providing plausible and imaginative defences of the basic civil institutions – private property, law, civil rights and contract – Hegel deals subtly with the more delicate features of political order, such as education, ceremony, welfare and the division of powers. He was not a democrat, although he advocated a representative parliament empowered to advise and correct the executive power. He believed that representation of the people was as much threatened by voting as sustained by it, and that it could exist only when mediated by constitutional provisions. The maintenance of these provisions requires the active cooperation of the majority, and this cooperation can never be secured in a condition of need. Hegel therefore advocated the creation of a welfare state. The state, he suggested, cannot stand in a personal relation to its citizens and at the same time remain indifferent to their needs. Although their needs are not rights they nevertheless define the duties of the sovereign power.

For Hegel, the free market – as the core institution of civil society – is the necessary instrument for the transfer of wealth. Moreover, he argued, there could be no security of the household, and no established order from generation to generation, without the accumulation of capital. Capitalism is therefore the inescapable consequence of the distinction between civil society and state, and the necessary instrument of social continuity. Unlike Marx, who saw capitalism as the cause of the bourgeois order, Hegel believed capitalism to be the effect of it. Similarly, he saw class distinctions as the by-product of free association and the society of corporations, without the oppressive overtones implied by subsequent socialist critics.

Hegel rescued the human individual from the philosophy of individualism. By seeing institutions and individuals in their true interdependence he stood against both the a priori abstractions of liberalism and the dangerous desire, which was to become a familiar part of socialist polemics, for an end to politics – a final goal of equality and freedom, in which power will no longer be necessary and no longer exerted. An understanding of the human individual as a social artefact shows inequality to be natural, power to be part of a complex good, and constraint to be a necessary ingredient in the only freedom that we can value. The *bürgerliche Gesellschaft* is neither historically transitory nor morally corrupt: it is simply the highest form of ethical existence, in which humankind's enduring but imperfect nature is realised to the full.

Hegel's influence on subsequent political philosophy owed more to his philosophy of history than to the theories expounded in *The Philosophy of Right*. His vision of the inevitable march of history from each epoch to the next, urged on by the same dialectic that governs the spirit in all its spheres, has been one of the most damaging of all philosophically inspired illusions, responsible for the quasi-religious belief in progress and the 'end of history', and inspiring the revolution fetishism of the Marxists (*Lectures on the Philosophy of History*, delivered in 1822, 1828 and 1830). Indeed, in so far as German-language philosophy is concerned, the nineteenth century after Hegel had little to offer in the way of conservatism, which was revived only in the early twentieth century, in the social and economic theories that flourished in Austria and Hungary.

The French contemporaries of Hegel include several thinkers who have been called conservatives, the two most notable being Chateaubriand and Maistre. And there is one French liberal whose importance to the conservative movement is not to be underestimated, and that is Alexis de Tocqueville, whose record of his journey in America – *Democracy in America* (1835) – is possibly the most influential book on the American settlement to have issued from the hand of a foreigner. A brief survey of these three writers will take the argument forward to the second half of the nineteenth century, when conservatism was defining itself against new opponents and new social upheavals.

The term 'reactionary' (French *réactionnaire*) emerged around the time of the Revolution, to denote those who wished to undo the whole project and to restore some part, maybe the greater part, of what had been swept away. The most articulate of the reactionaries, who also deserves a place in the history of conservatism, was the diplomat Joseph, Comte de Maistre (1753–1821), who defended the doctrine of the divine right of kings, and who believed that only a restoration of the Bourbon monarchy could set France and its people again on the path of righteous government. He saw the Revolution as a defiance of France's Christian heritage, and was a leading exponent of 'ultramontanism', the theological doctrine that favours the centralisation of the authority of the Roman Catholic Church in the papacy (i.e. the spiritual source 'beyond the mountains', meaning the Alps). Ultramontanism briefly triumphed in 1814, towards the end of Maistre's life, with the revival of its principal advocate, the Jesuit Order. For Maistre it was a way of calling the French to humility; it was a way the French could recognise that they cannot create their own system of law and government, but must bow to a higher authority.

Hence, in his *Essai sur le principe générateur des constitutions politiques* (1809), Maistre argued against what he saw as the fundamental error of all liberal theories, declaring that constitutions are not made but found, and that the rage for constitution-making which characterised the governments of his day was in part derived from a misconception of the American Constitution, which was no more than a document making explicit a spirit already present in the Anglo-American common law. All constitutions and all states are inseparable from the inner life of civil association; the attempt to separate the constitution from the unspoken spirit of the people means social and political death. For Maistre, obligation to the sovereign can have no basis in contract or consent, but only in piety towards established things. The true object of political obligation is not the state, but God, and it is in religious duty that the obligation towards all human institutions must ultimately be founded. Moreover it is God, and not man, who is the maker of constitutions, and the ultimate legislator, all French revolutionary thought on this subject being nothing but blasphemy designed to fortify human incompetence.

The Enlightenment, with its impious view of human perfectibility, was a collective manifestation of the sin of pride – an 'insurrection against God'. The violence of the Revolution was entirely what must be expected when people attempt to deny the reality of original sin and to take their destiny into their own hands. The events of the Terror were literally satanic, re-enacting the revolt of the fallen angels, and displaying what ensues when human beings reject the idea of authority, and imagine themselves capable of discovering a new form of government in the freedom from government.

Maistre's thoughts are brilliantly expressed, but with a certain remorseless extremism. Some among them are echoed in milder form by Hegel, who argues that 'the constitution should not be regarded as something made, even though it has come into being in time. It must be treated rather as something simply existent in and by itself, as divine therefore, and constant, and so as exalted above the sphere of things that are made' (*Philosophy of Right*, §273).

Again like Maistre, Hegel saw monarchy as the concrete embodiment and symbolic enactment of the individual personality of the state. In the person of the monarch, he wrote, 'the unity of the state is saved from the risk of being drawn down into the sphere of particularity and its caprices, ends and opinions, and saved too from the war of factions around the throne, and from the enfeeblement and over-throw of the power of the state'(§281). Hegel's arguments, absorbing the legitimist and monarchist claims into a fun-damentally forward-looking view of what is at stake, miti-gate what often seems, from the pen of Maistre, a hopelessly romantic evocation of forms of life that have gone forever, and perhaps never really existed. But Hegel's position comes close to Maistre's when he argues that it is dangerous to give utilitarian arguments for an institution whose authority depends, in the last analysis, upon simple piety. To offer consequential reasons for hereditary monarchy is 'to drag down the majesty of the throne into the sphere of argumen-tation, to ignore its true character as ungrounded imme-diacy and ultimate inwardness, and to base it not on the idea of the state immanent within it, but on something external to itself, on some extraneous notion such as "the welfare of the state" or "the welfare of the people" ' (§281).

Hegel was preparing the way for the emerging monar-chy of Prussia; Maistre was mourning the old monarchy of France. But while Hegel was a true conservative, developing a theory of sovereignty in which continuity, custom and free association were the roots of legitimate order, Maistre was lamenting what he saw as the Devil's work. He was recalling the French people to the religious faith that defined them, and saw political order and political institutions as legitimate only to the extent that they embodied and preserved the Christian heritage.

Ultramontanism remained a force in French conservatism throughout the nineteenth century, and hints of it can be discerned in the twentieth-century 'Catholic Revival' after the First World War. Joseph de Maistre's version might well be dismissed as reactionary; but it should be borne in mind that, in so far as conservatism arose in France, it was almost invariably connected with a reverence for the Catholic faith and for France as bearing witness to that faith. Moreover, there is an explanation of why French conservatives, in the wake of the Revolution, turned to their ancestral religion for inspiration, and it is an explanation that bears again on the difference between the American and the French revolutions.

The American Revolution led to a constitution that incorporated the results of debate and compromise, in which long-established customs and expectations were defined and endorsed. The US Constitution was not a panacea, or a comprehensive doctrine by which all life should be guided. It left the citizen in charge, free to adopt whatever way of life might conform to the purely negative constraints of the central government – and that was its greatest virtue. All this is contained in the famous first amendment, which affirms that 'Congress shall make no law respecting an establishment of religion, or prohibiting the free exercise thereof; or abridging the freedom of speech, or of the press; or the right of the people peaceably to assemble, and to petition the Government for a redress of grievances.'

The French revolutionaries, by contrast, offered a total doctrine, a comprehensive ideology, which competed directly with religion for the possession of the human soul. The church was the enemy, and priests were forced to swear loyalty to the Revolution in defiance of their holy vows. To combat the Revolution, therefore, it was necessary also to reclaim the spiritual territory that it had set out to conquer. Only a comprehensive doctrine, a complete vision of human destiny, could answer to the political need of the moment, and perforce that complete vision was the faith that the revolutionaries had set out to destroy, and which had remained in the hearts of the people despite all the sufferings that they had had to endure on its behalf.

Perhaps the most eloquent spokesman for this faith, and the one who saw most clearly that its restoration was bound up with the conservative project in politics, was François-René, Vicomte de Chateaubriand (1768–1848), one of the most remarkable literary and political figures of the first half of the nineteenth century, who made his name in the early 1800s as the author of exotic tales purporting to capture the spirit of the native American tribes, visited as a young man during a journey to America. A varied and romantic career, first as an émigré in London, then in diplomatic service to Napoleon, whom he turned from in disgust over the judicial murder of the Duc d'Enghien, and then as ambassador and briefly foreign minister under the Bourbon Restoration, did not distract Chateaubriand from his primary occupation as a writer of exquisite prose – his posthumous *Mémoires d'outre-tombe* is one of the great classics of Romantic literature.

Chateaubriand's principal contributions to French conservatism were twofold. First he wrote an extensive defence and advocacy of the Christian faith, published in 1802 as *Génie du Christianisme*, which was decisively to influence intellectuals of his generation away from the deism and agnosticism of the Enlightenment. Secondly, he showed in his life and his writings that conservatism was a kind of aesthetic and spiritual renewal – a way out from the dreary orthodoxies of revolutionary egalitarianism, into a world of romantic extravagance, sombre subjectivity and flamboyant style.

Out of Chateaubriand came not only French romanticism but also the first stirrings of the Gothic Revival, the movements towards the conservation of nature and the restoration of historic monuments, and the ready acceptance, after the Bourbon Restoration, of a mixed government in which aristocracy again had a decisive role. *Génie du Christianisme* was welcomed by Napoleon, since it coincided with his overtures to the papacy, and seemed to give strength to Napoleon's view that it is not the truth but the social utility of the Christian faith that matters. Although, unlike Napoleon, Chateaubriand was a believer, he described the faith as shining its radiance through all customs and institutions and endowing life with an aesthetic aura that could survive all merely intellectual doubts.

Christianity did not mean the belief in the incarnation and the resurrection only. It was manifest in ritual and rites of passage, in the ceremonies of church and state, in poetry, art, architecture, literature and music, in the religious life and the life of ordinary society. It was a kind of genius, a spirit that flowed through all things, remaking them as symbols of our spiritual salvation. And Chateaubriand expressed the point in prose that planted the message in the hearts of his contemporaries. David Cairns, in *Berlioz: The Making of an Artist, 1803–1832* (1989), aptly summarises the impact of Chateaubriand in these words:

> Beyond its specific purpose, *Génie du Christianisme* set a current of sympathy flowing between the author and a whole generation of young French men and women, kindling their imaginations over a wide range of feelings and ideas: the power of the great epic writers, Nature in its immense diversity and grandeur, the poetry of ruins, the spell of the distant past, the beauty of immemorial popular rituals and the haunting melancholy of the music accompanying them, the pangs of awakening consciousness and the perils and ardours of the solitary adolescent soul. More than any other work, it was the primer of early French Romanticism.

Comte Alexis de Tocqueville (1805–59), like Chateaubriand, made a journey, as a young man, to America, having been commissioned by King Louis Philippe to investigate the American penitentiary system. He travelled widely while there, exploring the reasons why the catastrophe that followed the French Revolution had not been visited on the Americans. The book that resulted from this journey, *Democracy in America* (1835), is a work of detached observation, remarkable for describing both the outward form of democratic politics and the inner life-world of the democratic citizen.

Tocqueville was profoundly influenced by Anglo-American liberalism, and regarded himself as being neither of the revolutionary nor of the conservative tendency when it came to politics in France. But he foresaw the triumph of the democratic spirit in Europe and wished to prepare his countrymen so that they might seize the good parts of it and refuse the bad. In particular, he wished to sound a warning against putting equality above liberty in the scheme of ultimate values.

For the 'principle of equality', whereby all distinctions of social status are gradually eroded, threatened to become the motor of modern history. The tendency towards equality had, Tocqueville thought, been present since the Middle Ages and, with the American and French revolutions, had entered its final stage. The major problem facing modern society, according to Tocqueville, is that of reconciling equality with liberty, in the increasing absence of the diversity of power that had characterised traditional aristocratic regimes. The lower classes undermine the upper by increasing centralisation, which erodes all social hierarchy, regionalism and local feeling, and results in an unprecedented concentration of power in the state. Nevertheless, in a prescient and in many ways laudatory account of the US Constitution, Tocqueville acknowledged that the American system encouraged decentralised government, even in a condition of complete democracy. He also praised the Constitution as embodying democratic expectations, while retaining the mechanisms by which the blunderings of democratic politics could be corrected.

Tocqueville described the Anglo-American trial by jury

as a political system, acting out the sovereignty of the people in the courtroom; and he saw judicial independence in the US as endowing the judiciary with some of the stabilising influence and inherent political privilege of the European aristocracy. Thanks to these institutions the worst effects of the obsession with equality had been avoided.

Tocqueville also warned against what he called 'democratic despotism', when majority sentiment gathers strength sufficient to override the rights of minorities. The political pursuit of equality breeds loss of individuality, self-assurance and social ease, and therefore tends towards uniformity, and begins to see the eccentric as a threat. Not only liberty but also culture and intellectual distinction are threatened by the equalising process; class distinctions begin to be replaced by increasingly arbitrary-seeming distinctions of status, without the dignifying attributes of culture and leisure that might otherwise have led to their acceptance.

The 'imperfect phantom of equality' haunts the mind of all, destroying obedience, honour and the capacity to command, so that people, increasingly unable to find solace in the social order, will be confined within the solitude of their hearts. To some extent this tendency to fragmentation is countered by the American genius for association, which leads to a proliferation of clubs, churches and societies in which long-standing and genial hierarchies are recreated. In this way Tocqueville discovered in America the 'little platoons' that had been so ruthlessly destroyed by the Jacobins in France.

In *The Old Regime and the French Revolution* (1856),

Tocqueville gave a highly influential account of the causes and effects of the French Revolution, arguing that revolutions occur when things begin to improve, or when things go wrong after a period of improvement – a view that many have seen confirmed in subsequent history. Although revolution speeds up the real change, that change – towards centralisation, bureaucracy, and the increasing levelling of social hierarchy – is not caused by revolution but precedes it, being itself one of the major causes of radicalisation, since it undermines the old privileges which made preventive measures possible. Tocqueville blamed the old aristocracy for much of its loss of power; it had become a caste and, unlike the English gentry, had been willing to exchange political power for social exclusiveness and fiscal privilege, thus becoming both obnoxious to the majority, and unable to defend itself.

In their several ways Maistre, Chateaubriand and Tocqueville all reject some aspect of the Enlightenment – popular sovereignty in Maistre's case, secularism in Chateaubriand's and egalitarianism in Tocqueville's. While sharing the revolutionaries' desire for a complete vision of human destiny, they were all three passionate critics of the French Revolution and its nihilistic legacy that had permitted the rise of Napoleon. Thereafter conservatism in France pursued a bumpy passage through the successive monarchies and republics until the simultaneous rise of aggressive German nationalism and French republican socialism entirely transformed its agenda. But the new mission of conservatism, as a systematic response to socialism, did not take proper shape until the end of the nineteenth century.

Other concerns occupied the conservative mind during the second half of the nineteenth century, as societies rapidly moved from agrarian to industrial forms of production. This development returns us to the Anglosphere, and in particular to England, where the Industrial Revolution first made itself felt.

# 4

# CULTURAL CONSERVATISM

Between 1688 and 1832 Britain enjoyed what was, by European standards, a rare period of stability, with internal order disturbed only by the short-lived Jacobite Rebellions. During this time the country underwent large constitutional changes, including the Acts of Union with Scotland and Ireland, the final removal of the disabilities suffered by Catholics (the Roman Catholic Relief Act, 1829), and the extension of the franchise in the Reform Act of 1832. The Reform Act led to the creation of political parties, the Conservative Party included, and thereafter extension of the franchise became a fixed item on the political agenda.

By and large those developments can be seen as the steady move towards the popular sovereignty advocated by Enlightenment liberalism. But the stability needed to bring them about depended on the growing prosperity of the country, through trade overseas and industrialisation at home. Both factors changed Great Britain utterly. Overseas trade led to the growth of an empire, acquired, as the historian Sir John Robert Seeley famously put it, 'in a fit of absence of mind', and with it a new kind of multinational sovereignty;[6] industrialisation led to vast demographic changes, as the population moved from the countryside into the towns and the towns grew to receive them.

6   *The Expansion of England*, London, 1883.

In this way there entered on to the stage of world history its most talked-about protagonist, the 'working class'. At first this was composed of people uprooted from the land, employed in large workforces on factory floors and living in towns that made little provision for their social and spiritual needs. Within a few decades, however, the working class had settlements of its own, had created around itself a culture and a sense of identity, was demanding representation in Parliament, and had acquired a champion in the Chartist movement. Social theories explaining this class, and political doctrines defending it, now took up position in the centre of contemporary debates, and in the course of the nineteenth century these theories and doctrines came together in the socialist movement. By the turn of the twentieth century it was no longer against liberalism that conservatism was defining itself, but against socialism, and in particular against the socialist conception of the state.

Meanwhile, however, another form of conservatism was emerging, one that did not have political institutions and the powers of government as its primary subject matter but which focused instead on culture. One of the effects of the population transfers of the late eighteenth and early nineteenth centuries was to detach people from their religious and social roots, and thereby to dethrone the Anglican Church, which was and had always been a predominantly rural institution. Non-conformist chapels sprang up in the towns, while the calls for Catholic Emancipation intensified, in the wake of the Act of Union with Ireland of 1800, which gave the largely Catholic population of Ireland the same political status as the English, the Welsh and the Scots.

Belatedly, British writers began to address the great questions that had animated Chateaubriand – the questions of the place of Christianity in civil society, and of the relation between church and state.

This occurred at a time when the movement for radical reform had moved in a new direction, away from liberalism towards the advocacy of comprehensive social plans. Even the opponents of the French Revolution could not fail to observe that old things were being rapidly swept away by the Industrial Revolution, and that old institutions were ever more in need of reform if the changes in civil society were to be accommodated. In France the fashion grew for far-reaching, often utopian, programmes for the government of human societies, wherever and whenever they might have arisen. These no longer mentioned individual liberty as the primary political value, but advocated 'reason' and 'progress' instead – progress towards a community of sharing, as advocated by François Marie Charles Fourier (1772–1837), or towards a society reorganised from top to bottom on socialist principles, as in the writings of Claude-Henri de Rouvroy, Comte de Saint-Simon (1760–1825). These progressivist views were assimilated into a kind of secular religion by Saint-Simon's secretary, August Comte (1798–1857), the inventor of the term 'sociology', and the founder of the church of Positivism.

A similar, though milder, shift occurred in Britain, away from liberalism towards the new philosophy of 'utilitarianism', which proposed happiness, rather than liberty, as the goal of both morality and law. Its chief exponent, Jeremy Bentham (1748–1832), was an opponent of the liberal idea of natural rights, and argued that laws should be justified by their effect in promoting general happiness, of which he gave a quaint and quantitative picture. His *Introduction to the Principles of Morals and Legislation* (1789) became the bible for a new species of political reformers, among them James Mill (1773–1836), leader of the self-styled 'philosophical radicals', and James's son, the liberal philosopher John Stuart Mill (1806–73).

In the early decades of the nineteenth century, therefore, conservative-minded thinkers no longer addressed liberalism or popular sovereignty as their targets. Anxieties over the loss of religious roots, over the dehumanising effect of the Industrial Revolution and the damage done to the old and settled way of life, together with revulsion towards the new forms of 'progressive' opinion, which seemed to treat all questions of morality and law as mathematical puzzles, to be solved by calculation – all these created a sense that something precious was at risk as the new century unfolded. Thus arose a movement within intellectual conservatism that proposed culture as both the remedy to the loneliness and alienation of industrial society, and the thing most under threat from the new advocates of social reform. The movement began with Coleridge and continued through John Ruskin and Matthew Arnold down to T. S. Eliot and F. R. Leavis in twentieth-century Britain, and the contemporaneous 'Southern Agrarians' in America.

The poet Samuel Taylor Coleridge (1772–1834) made one of the first attempts to adapt the philosophical vision of Kant and the early German idealists to the evaluation of the social condition of England, thereby taking a stand against

what he saw as the fragmented vision of society characteristic of British empiricism. He was particularly hostile to
the utilitarian theories of Bentham, and argued that human
values cannot be understood by what Bentham called the
'felicific calculus', which measures the value of our actions
in terms of the pleasure and pain that result from them.
Coleridge rejected the idea of human progress as a linear
movement propelled by scientific knowledge, and felt that
the enlightened rationalism of his contemporaries ignored
the instinctive relations between people that form the true
bond of society.

In this way Coleridge was close to Chateaubriand,
searching for the spirit that had been embodied in religion
and which Enlightenment ways of thinking had chased
from its many shrines. He was among the first in a long
line of British thinkers who have advocated government
intervention in the economy in order to relieve poverty,
to provide education and to give a share of the collective
prosperity to those who have, through no fault of their own,
been deprived of it. In this way he set the agenda for those
subsequent cultural conservatives who opposed unbridled
free market economics.

Coleridge defended the institutions of Anglicanism and,
in *On the Constitution of the Church and State* (1830), strove
to reconcile the demands of political order and constitution
with the more instinctive needs that are embodied in religious institutions. Here, as elsewhere, he defended the view
that culture is an indispensable mediator between explicit
law and implicit social feeling, and argued for the political
importance of the 'clerisy', or learned class, in whom the

culture of a nation is enshrined, and who, in taking decisions informed by that culture, act in tune with the deeper,
unspoken instincts of the people:

> The clerisy of a nation, or national church, in its primary
> acceptation and original intention, comprehended the
> learned of all denominations; – the sages and professors
> of the law and jurisprudence; of medicine and physiology,
> of music; of military and civil architecture; of the physical
> sciences; with the mathematical as the common *organ* of the
> preceding; in short, all the so-called liberal arts and sciences,
> the possession of which constitutes the civilization of a
> country, as well as the theological.

That passage illustrates both the impulsive nature of
Coleridge's thinking, and also his distinctively modern
faith in the role of the intellectual, for whom he was the first
true propagandist in Britain, despite his somewhat medieval conception of the established church. His arguments
for the indispensability of culture shaped many of the nineteenth-century expressions of cultural conservatism, and
also awoke J. S. Mill to the shortcomings of the utilitarian
creed. Coleridge's importance lies partly in his attempt to
lean on German idealism, rather than British empiricism, in
formulating a full picture of the political life. Unfortunately,
although he read and was puzzled by Hegel's *Logic*, he does
not seem to have come across the *Philosophy of Right*, which
might have clarified his intellectual goals.

The agenda of cultural conservatism becomes clearer in
the writings of its greatest British exponent, John Ruskin
(1819–1900), the writer, painter and social critic, who presented a highly wrought and conflicted view of the Christian

inheritance and its irreplaceable value. It is to Ruskin that modern conservation societies such as the National Trust and the Society for the Preservation of Ancient Buildings owe their original inspiration, and his fine descriptions of the spiritual meaning of just about everything he set his eyes upon mark him out as the high priest of the aesthetic way of life.

Ruskin began his literary career with striking books on painting and architecture, including *Modern Painters* (1843–60) and *The Stones of Venice* (1851–3). But already those works announced his true vocation as a social critic and moralist. Ruskin saw in the art of the past a spiritual wholeness and social cohesion which were, he believed, vanishing from the world of industrial capitalism. All that is most valuable in life depends upon transcending the motive of profit and the spirit of calculation. The machine age had degraded work into a means; it had also done the same for leisure – and therefore for art. For medieval craftsmen, work was an act of piety and was sanctified in their own eyes as in the eyes of their God. For such labourers, end and means are one and the spiritual wholeness of faith is translated into the visual wholeness and purity of their craft. Hence their craft was also art, a permanent testimony to the reality on earth of humanity's spiritual redemption.

From such ideas Ruskin mounted a sustained and passionate defence of the Gothic Revival in architecture, denouncing almost all the buildings of his day as unfeeling products of the profit machine. He was fervently anti-utilitarian and anti-capitalist, and yet he distanced himself from socialism, writing dismissively of the egalitarian and materialistic values which socialists espouse. It is perhaps more accurate to describe Ruskin (as he described himself) as a Tory – though of a highly peculiar and romantic kind, a Protestant version of Chateaubriand, but manifestly without the Frenchman's immense sexual prowess. (Ruskin's tormented view of women, focusing on their untouchable purity and preciousness and therefore on their hidden reality as children, is responsible for some of the more toe-curling passages of his prose.)

Ruskin's ideas came from art, and from brilliant insights into the moral and spiritual significance of the aesthetic enterprise. But he applied these ideas in the social sphere with an uncompromising elitism. His social writings are really lay sermons exhorting his countrymen to Christian morality and pious works and to the acceptance of a faith in which he himself only half believed. He wrote intensely (and to a feminist, shockingly) on the differences between the sexes (*Sesame and Lilies*, 1865), and regarded the working classes as more in need of a statement of their duties than a list of their rights (*Fors Clavigera*, a series of 'letters to the workmen and labourers of Great Britain', published during the 1870s). His carefully honed style borders at times on sentimentality, and expresses in its every rhythm a deep sense of disappointment with the human species, together with a memory of the angelic visions from which his life began.

Many accuse conservatism of being no more than a highly wrought work of mourning, a translation into the language of politics of the yearning for childhood that lies deep in us all. Ruskin's prose gives some substance to that accusation. Fortunately, however, he is not the only or even the most recognised advocate of cultural conservatism in the face of the modern economy and the modern state. His contemporary, the poet Matthew Arnold (1822–88), was an exponent of cultural conservatism who manifestly did not deceive himself that the faith from which our culture ultimately derives could be restored in anything like the form that gave rise to the enchanted world of the Gothic cathedral. In his great poem 'Dover Beach' (1867) he refers to the 'Sea of Faith' and its 'melancholy, long, withdrawing roar', suggesting that modern people must find from their own resources, and in particular from personal love, the way to maintain the inner order on which external stability depends. It is precisely for this, Arnold believed, that we should esteem the legacy of culture, which provides us with the social knowledge that we need, whether or not we have the religious faith with which to back it up.

In *Culture and Anarchy* (1869), Arnold defined culture as 'a pursuit of our total perfection by means of getting to know, on all matters which most concern us, the best which has been thought and said in the world, and, through this knowledge, turning a stream of fresh and free thought upon our stock notions and habits'. Arnold argued that culture, and access to culture, were essential for the right direction of political power, and that, without them, there could be no true conception of the ends of human conduct, but only a mechanistic obsession with the means. He criticised many of the 'stock notions' of nineteenth-century liberalism and utilitarianism, on account of their materialist, rationalist and individualist visions of human progress.

The concept of freedom upon which so much liberal thought depends seemed to Arnold to be too abstract – 'a very good horse to ride, but to ride somewhere' – and to contain no serious reasons for opposing the state in its name. The state, he argued, is 'the representative acting-power of the nation', and therefore must have power to act both in the name of freedom, and in the name of order. Without it, public life must always be diverted towards the interests of one or other class, of which Arnold distinguished three, the 'barbarians' or aristocracy, the 'philistines' or middle class, and the 'populace' or working class. When this happens, the result is anarchy; however, within each class there is a spirit opposed to anarchy, and dedicated to the common good and public order: this is the spirit that culture awakens, nourishes and refines. To achieve political order, therefore, the state must guarantee the transmission of culture, which means that humane education must be as widely available as possible.

Arnold was for part of his life inspector of schools, during that crucial time when provisions were being put in place for a universal educational system. He shared the conviction of his father, Thomas Arnold, the famous headmaster of Rugby, that social order depends on 'character' and that character is what a school is really about. Matthew regarded the utilitarian and technological attitude of the 'philistines' – which is to say the owners of property, the captains of industry and the bureaucrats – as a threat to long-term social harmony, since it erodes the sense of intrinsic value. True education restores that sense by introducing the student to 'the best that has been thought and said' in the art, literature and scholarship of mankind. Although Arnold's conservatism repeated Burke's strictures against individualism, and emphasised social continuity and tradition in terms not dissimilar from Burke's, his real target was not liberalism so much as the mechanistic belief in material 'progress' and the utilitarian values of the new breed of social reformers.

By the time that Ruskin and Arnold wrote, the vast demographic and economic changes of the Victorian era were well under way, and with the 1867 Representation of the People Act large sections of the working class were to obtain the vote. By and large conservative thinkers accepted the extension of the franchise, and it was a conservative politician, the novelist and twice elected prime minister Benjamin Disraeli, Earl of Beaconsfield (1804–81), who was responsible for seeing the change through Parliament, in furtherance of the philosophy expounded in the preface to his novel *Sybil, or The Two Nations* (1845). Here, Disraeli wrote of the division of the kingdom into the owners of the factories and the people who worked in them, and of the need to unite the classes in the 'one nation' that they share. On the whole, cultural conservatives shared Disraeli's reservations about industrial capitalism and his belief that active intervention from the state is needed in order to relieve the condition of the poor. Nevertheless, they clung to the belief in things of the mind – education, art and aesthetic values – and for all of them it was beauty and not utility that stood at the top of the political agenda.

This led to an interesting paradox, evident too in the cultural conservatives of the twentieth century. Cultural conservatism originated in the experience of a way of life that was under threat or disappearing. The memory of that way of life could be preserved, and its spiritual meaning enshrined in works of art. But the way of life itself could not be so easily protected. Should we then appeal to the state to subsidise a dying lifestyle, establishing wildlife parks like those in Aldous Huxley's *Brave New World*, in which the agrarian way of life stumbles on, unconscious of the world that lies beyond its sensitively policed perimeter? Or should we devote ourselves, instead, to the *idea* of the thing that we are bound to lose, keeping it alive in art, as did Strauss and von Hofmannsthal in perpetuating the sugar-coated seductiveness of the aristocratic life in *Der Rosenkavalier*, or D. H. Lawrence in celebrating the close-knit cohesion of the old mining communities in *Sons and Lovers*? But then, to whom will such works of art be addressed? Necessarily, to those who have become conscious of the old way of life as something lost, something that can be preserved only in this aesthetic form. For its practitioners it would have meant nothing to preserve their way of life as an *idea*, rather than as the reality of their being in the world. To put it more severely: culture becomes an object of conservation only when it has already been lost.

But then, isn't it the tradition of reflection on our way of life – the art, literature and music through which we make a bid for permanence – that is the real thing that we value? Isn't it this that we wish to preserve from the philistines, the utilitarians and the progressives, whose empty materialism threatens to turn us away from our true spiritual inheritance? Isn't it here, in the realm of 'high culture', that the battle must be fought? It is by pondering such questions, it seems to me, that the cause of cultural conservatism was advanced, becoming a battle over the curriculum, and an attempt to retrieve the thoughts and feelings that had been distilled in it.

The transfer of attention from politics to artistic practice is by no one better exemplified than by the Anglo-American poet Thomas Stearns Eliot (1888–1965), whose poems, plays and essays had a transforming effect on conservative philosophy in the twentieth century. Eliot was a modernist in literature, who did more than any other contemporary writer to rescue English poetry from its late Victorian archaisms and return it to the mainstream of European literature. He developed a laconic and allusive style, much influenced by Baudelaire, Laforgue and French symbolism, but addressed directly to the spiritual crisis, as he saw it, of modern civilisation. In *The Waste Land* (1922), Eliot evokes the barren soulscape of the city, summoning the feelings of loss and emptiness that followed the hollow victory of the First World War, and providing an unforgettable image of a place, a civilisation and a society suspended in the void and without clear hope of renewal. The poem appeared in the first issue of *The Criterion*, a journal founded in London by Eliot to propagate his distinctive vision of literature. Through this vision he remade the canon of English classics and entirely changed educated perception of what matters in the literature of the past.

Although *The Waste Land* invokes a condition of spiritual desolation, it does so in terms that are saturated with religious and literary allusions, creating a sense that this desolation is perceivable only because there is something else – an ideal order, a state of spiritual fulfilment, and an artistic tradition that embodies those things – through which it can be perceived and perhaps even renewed. In due course Eliot was drawn towards the Anglo-Catholic religion, became an articulate apologist for the doctrine and ritual of the Anglican Church, and defended a kind of retreat into high culture as the spiritual resource with which to combat the godlessness of modern society. In *The Idea of a Christian Society*, published on the eve of the Second World War in 1939, Eliot outlined the social structures and institutions that would be necessary if European civilisation were to turn back from the brink of total destruction and once again embrace its Christian inheritance, which he held to be the only guarantee of European survival. And in *Four Quartets* (1943), he presents a quasi-monastic vision in verse of enormous power, which helped to shape conservative thinking in the decades following the war. One message of the poem is that the spiritual tradition that in our daily lives seems dead and buried persists in sacred places and symbols. It is a kind of revelation of the nation and of our own social membership, and by opening our hearts to it, and allowing the present moment to fill with the residue of time past, we recuperate what we might have lost.

Cultural conservatism promoted the study, through literature, of the larger problems of definition that conservatives had encountered in their century-long attempt to become conscious of their own message. Concepts that seem hopelessly obscure or diverse when applied in the forum of political debate – concepts like tradition, order, realism, sincerity – have a function too in literary criticism, where they can be provided with examples, and their value explored. Orthodoxy, which so often seems like a wavering path in the political landscape, has a clear itinerary in literature, and concepts of centrality and authority, so necessary to conservatism in every sphere, have a clear application in the world of art, where Bach, Michelangelo, Tolstoy and Shakespeare set standards that cannot be denied or ignored.

Thus in a celebrated essay, 'Tradition and the Individual Talent' (1919), collected in *The Sacred Wood* (1921), Eliot argued that the originality and sincerity demanded of the artist cannot be reached in isolation, that each new work acquires its expressive power through the tradition that makes room for it, and that in every sphere tradition is a process of continuous adaptation of the old to the new and the new to the old. Without tradition, originality is neither significant nor truly perceivable, and this evolutionary view of tradition is clearly applicable to civil society as a whole. This essay left a profound mark on literary criticism and also on the practice of poetry. But its lesson has been learned and repeated by political philosophers too.

Cultural conservatives were for a while a commanding presence in English literary life, openly at war with the 'progressives', such as George Bernard Shaw, who dismissed them as nostalgic cranks. Among their important works are defences of Christianity from G. K. Chesterton (*Orthodoxy*, 1908, *The Everlasting Man*, 1925) and C. S. Lewis (*Mere Christianity*, 1952, based on wartime radio talks). Some of the flavour of Chesterton can be gleaned from his apt response to the progressive socialism of Shaw:

After belabouring a great many people for a great many years for being unprogressive, Mr. Shaw has discovered, with characteristic sense, that it is very doubtful whether any existing human being with two legs can be progressive at all. Having come to doubt whether humanity can be combined with progress, most people, easily pleased, would have elected to abandon progress and remain with humanity. Mr. Shaw, not being easily pleased, decides to throw over humanity with all its limitations and go in for progress for its own sake. If man, as we know him, is incapable of the philosophy of progress, Mr. Shaw asks, not for a new kind of philosophy, but for a new kind of man. It is rather as if a nurse had tried a rather bitter food for some years on a baby, and on discovering that it was not suitable, should not throw away the food and ask for a new food, but throw the baby out of the window, and ask for a new baby. (*Heretics*, 1905)

It was in the wake of Eliot's literary achievement that the most recent wave of cultural conservatism swept across British education. This was the work of a literary critic, F. R. Leavis (1895–1978) who, through the journal *Scrutiny*, which he founded in 1933, and such works as *Education and the University* (1943), advocated the teaching of English as a counter-measure to the 'technologico-Benthamite' ways of thinking that had, since the Industrial Revolution, so damaged the cultural inheritance of the country. The subject of English, conceived not merely as a study of the language and its freight of instinctive culture, but as a wide-ranging critical reflection on the 'Great Tradition' of English literature, should be the centre of humane education. It would offer the student a path back to the organic community that the utilitarians and the scholars had conspired to marginalise, and would open the hearts of young people to what is really at stake in the modern world, which is the persistence of 'felt life', as Henry James described it: the commodity to be found in such abundance in the great works of our tradition. True literature does not palm off on the reader a sentimental substitute for life in the manner (as Leavis supposed) of popular culture, but offers life itself, sincere, direct and imbued with the spirit of the soil.

Leavis was not a religious person, was suspicious of Eliot's later turn towards the Anglo-Catholic faith, and refused categorically to describe himself as a conservative. There is no doubt, however, that his crucial writings – *New Bearings in English Poetry* (1932), *Revaluation* (1946), and *The Great Tradition* (1948) – touched the same nerve as did Coleridge, Ruskin, Arnold and Eliot. The effect of those writings on a generation of English and Scottish schoolteachers was enormous, and 'Leavism' became, for a while, a recognisable movement in British schools. The Leavisite schoolteacher was severe in his judgements, easily shocked by any deviation from orthodoxy, urgently communicating a kind of puritanical vision of the common people and their culture, and upholding Bunyan, Wordsworth and D. H. Lawrence as the spokesmen for the real inheritance of the English-speaking lands.

For all its importance in Britain and its empire, however, cultural conservatism was not confined to the Anglosphere. The reaction against the Enlightenment was felt throughout Europe, and in the German-speaking countries of central Europe led to the first stirrings of the romantic nationalism that was to dominate cultural life by the mid-nineteenth century. The leading figure here is the philosopher and critic Johann Gottfried von Herder (1744–1803), who is the true originator of the Leavisite view of language, as encapsulating the common experiences and historical identity of a people.

In 1762, as a teenager, Herder had attended Kant's lectures in Königsberg, and he wrote partly in reaction to the philosopher's liberal view of political order. For Kant, Enlightenment was the moment of mankind's moral maturity, when the free individual emerges from the prison of custom and superstition. Guided by the light of reason, such an individual will adopt the universal moral law that reason commands. Kant's argument for this position did not persuade Herder, who believed that it gave too thin a description of the moral motive, reducing human beings to their over-civilised shadows. For Herder there was a deep distinction in the human psyche between Civilisation, which is the sphere of rational calculation and institution building, and Culture, which is the shared temperament of a *Volk*. Culture is what unites human beings in mutual attachment, and consists of language, custom, folk tales and folk religion.

In the course of expounding that idea Herder proposed medieval Germany as a cultural icon in the place of the hitherto adopted classical Greek ideal (*Ideas on the Philosophy of the History of Mankind,* 1784–91). He also began the practice of collecting and publishing folk poetry and folk tales, and thereby inspired the subsequent work of Achim von Arnim and Clemens Brentano (*Des Knaben Wunderhorn,* 1805–8) and the folk-tale collections of the Brothers Grimm (1812).

Herder was a Protestant clergyman, and his romantic nationalism was inseparable from his attachment to Martin Luther's Bible, the great work that taught ordinary Germans to read, and that endowed their language with its lasting spiritual resonance. Herder regretted that Luther had not founded a national church, which would have provided durable foundations to a unified German culture. Subsequent nationalist writers saw national sentiment more as an alternative to religion than a form of it, and recognised that Luther had been as much responsible for the divisions among the German people as for the language that united them. Very soon the cultural conservatism initiated by Herder had become a kind of political radicalism, influencing the revolutions of 1848, in which the Germans laid claim to a shared identity within boundaries that would bring them together as a single nation state. This subsequent history lies beyond the horizon of this book. But it is worth noting that German nationalism, however radical it became in political terms, owed its original inspiration to the very same cultural conservatism that led in Britain to the Gothic Revival and the National Trust, and in France to the flamboyant romanticism of Chateaubriand and the restoration of a Catholic countryside.

In America the story is somewhat different. The division between the Southern and the Northern states of the Union, which came to a head in the civil war, but which had deep roots in the history of colonisation, was associated with conflicting ideas of the American settlement. The entrepreneurial and puritan culture of Massachusetts was pitted against the feudal and aristocratic order of Jefferson's

Virginia, and when cultural conservatism came into being during the nineteenth century its focus was on the agrarian way of life that Jefferson had wished to conserve as the foundation of a settled political order. When Northern writers and philosophers stepped back from the world of material progress it was often, like Henry David Thoreau (1817–62), to take refuge in solitude. Nature, as described in Thoreau's *Walden* (1854), is not the settled farmstead and plantation house of Jefferson, but the wilderness, the place where you are alone with your soul. There, communing with nature, the philosopher can envisage the 'equable life', which is one of 'simplicity, magnanimity and trust'. Institutions are by no means necessary to this form of life, for in everything we should strive for a heroic independence – such is the message that rises with the mist from Walden Pond, and it is a message that repudiates the rural settlements that inspired the Jeffersonian vision of political order.

Cultural conservatism became a real force in American civil society only in the twentieth century, when a group of twelve writers, defining themselves as Southern Agrarians, joined together to publish a manifesto, *I'll Take My Stand* (1930), under the unofficial leadership of the poet John Crowe Ransom (1888–1974), then teaching at Vanderbilt University in Nashville, Tennessee. In so far as the manifesto had any shared political vision it was captured in the introduction to the volume, which argued that 'the theory of agrarianism is that the culture of the soil is the best and most sensitive of vocations, and that therefore it should have the economic preference and enlist the maximum number of workers.'

Vague as a statement of policy, the manifesto neverthe-less engaged with the profound feelings of loss experienced in the Southern states. The writers believed that the rapid urbanisation of America, the growth of the cities, and the speeding up of all human encounters by the media of mass communication and the motorcar, had detached Americans so completely from the soil that they were no longer at home in their own country. And some of them ventured explicitly to declare their sorrow at the outcome of the civil war, which had led first to the misrepresentation of the Southern way of life, and then to the extinction of that way of life by the industrial culture of the North. Those senti-ments found poignant expression in a poem by Allen Tate, 'Ode to the Confederate Dead' (1937), and when Tate served as co-editor of the long-standing *Sewanee Review* from 1942 to 1944 the journal became an active voice in defence of a wished-for agrarian civilisation. It was active in conscript-ing literary criticism in the fight for traditional values and traditional forms of community, and published works by the leading cultural conservative Richard Weaver. Weaver's melancholy résumé of the decline of Western civilisation, in *Ideas Have Consequences* (1948), traces that decline as far back as the Middle Ages, when the nominalism of William of Ockham began to undermine the old authorities and put the individual in charge.

Wild generalisations (such as that one), illusions about the real causality of ideas, futile nostalgia for a lost order of things, not to speak of a failure to come to grips with slavery and its legacy – all these faults have been pinned on the cultural conservatives of the South. Nevertheless, their vision achieved poignant and moving expression in both poetry and prose, with names like Allen Tate, Eudora Welty, Flannery O'Connor and Robert Penn Warren remaining prominent in the pantheon of modern American literature. The influence of their stance is still felt, not least in the environmental movement and those members of it, such as Wendell Berry and Allan C. Carlson, who cherish in their hearts the life and culture of the family farm. Significant in this connection are Allan Carlson's updating of the Agrarian stance in *The New Agrarian Mind: The Movement Toward Decentralist Thought in Twentieth-Century America* (2000), and Wendell Berry's *The Unsettling of America: Culture and Agriculture* (1977).

Cultural conservatism, of a kind, is also responsible for what has been perhaps the most influential *academic* approach to conservatism in America, namely the school of political science associated with Leo Strauss (1899–1973), who came to the United States as a refugee from Nazism in 1937 and who, after a variety of academic posts, settled in the University of Chicago. Strauss's example as a teacher, given to close readings of great texts in the manner of German philology, was influential in establishing American political science as a humane discipline and part of the core curriculum in the academy.

Strauss was influenced by his study of ancient philosophy (especially Plato), by the radical German constitutional theorist Carl Schmitt (1888–1986), and also by his reading of the US Constitution and the thinking that created it. His own views were unsystematic, but involved a defence of the rule of law and the balance of interests achieved by the US Constitution. He was opposed to 'historicism', by which he meant the habit of referring all ideas to the historical context from which they arose. Political science, he believed, must aim for the trans-historical perspective, from which ideas could be judged for their validity. Strauss believed that he had found that perspective in the idea of natural rights, which he understood in the sense of Locke and the American Declaration of Independence.

Even if historicism is the enemy of political science, however, Strauss believed that in studying the classics of political theory it is always necessary to 'read between the lines' in order to discover the rhetorical goal of the writer. Political theory is itself part of politics, and politics is the sphere in which people can achieve, by painstaking and arduous means, the accommodation required for their common fulfilment. Strauss deplored the fascist, communist and socialist movements that were tearing Europe apart, and deplored equally the failure of American intellectuals to appreciate the profound thinking behind their own legal, political and social institutions, and the fact that these things are far more easily lost than won.

Much American political science has been stamped with Strauss's brand of conservatism, so that the adjective 'Straussian' has acquired a distinct sense in the world of political theory – meaning roughly conservative, constitutionalist, and rooted in deep readings of the classics (readings, however, which expose the complexity and ambiguity of the author's real intentions). Strauss's many distinguished pupils include Allan Bloom (who briefly features in Chapter 6, below). Strauss's achievement, in founding a school of political science within the American academy, has had repercussions outside the academy, with 'Straussians' obtaining influential positions in government and administration under the conservative presidency of George W. Bush. This in turn has led to an industry of scholarship devoted to exposing Strauss as a malign and perverse influence, responsible for neo-conservatism (see Chapter 6), tort reform, and the war in Iraq.

Cultural conservatism, in all its forms, has been an attempt to lift conservatism from the battleground of politics into the peaceful arena of literature and academic life. It has been apprehensive of mass culture, democratic politics, and the new 'progressive' doctrines for the redemption of mankind. It has retreated from modernity to the tranquil pastures of the mind, where education, knowledge and high culture have an insuperable advantage over majority opinion and politicised ignorance. In the classroom, at least, it seems possible to win, on the understanding that ideas are respected there. But what happens when the tide of socialist opinion sweeps through the classroom too? What remains of conservatism, when it is driven into a corner in its last redoubt? This is a question to which I shall briefly return in the final chapter. Before that, we need to explore the confrontation between conservatism and the socialist state, a confrontation that revised and extended the arguments of Smith, Burke and Hegel and once again made political philosophy central to the history of the West.

# 5

# THE IMPACT OF SOCIALISM

By the end of the First World War the cultural conservatism sketched in the previous chapter had ceased to provide a coherent political programme. The old civilisation of Europe, with its supposedly organic rural society and Christian high culture, was widely distrusted as a guide to the future. It had become a faded idea, not to be exposed to the glare of politics, but to be carefully unfolded from time to time like a precious parchment in the literary twilight. Nowhere was this more evident than in the former Austro-Hungarian Empire, where the war had started, and where the old order of things had collapsed entirely after the German and Austrian defeat. There emerged in Vienna and its former dependencies thereafter a literature of mourning that is without compare in modern times. Works like Stefan Zweig's *The World of Yesterday*, which Zweig began in 1934, Robert Musil's *The Man Without Qualities*, published posthumously in 1940, or Joseph Roth's *The Radetzky March* (1932), invoke a precious social order that was also an order in the soul, while in Rainer Maria Rilke's *Duino Elegies*, published in 1923, but already partly conceived in 1912, we find the greatest attempt in modern literature to discover meaning in the inner life, when the props of society and religion have been removed and only the 'I' remains, miraculously standing like a lone steeple above the ruins of all that once surrounded it.

Notwithstanding the disasters of the twentieth century, and in part because of them, that kind of cultural conservatism has continued to attract some of the best minds of Europe and America, remaining a vigorous if melancholy force in contemporary art and literature. But by the end of the nineteenth century the political philosophy of conservatism had turned in another direction. In its original form, as described in the first two chapters, conservatism was a response to classical liberalism, a kind of 'yes, but ...' in answer to the 'yes' of popular sovereignty. It was a defence of inheritance against radical innovation, an insistence that the liberation of the individual could not be achieved without the maintenance of customs and institutions that were threatened by the single-minded emphasis on freedom and equality. By the end of the nineteenth century conservatism had begun to define itself in another way, as a response to the gargantuan schemes for a 'just' society, to be promoted by the new kind of managerial state. In this battle conservatism became, to a great measure, the true defender of liberty, against what was at best a rising system of bureaucratic government, at worst, as in the Soviet Union, a tyranny yet more murderous than that of the Jacobins in revolutionary France.

In the course of the confrontation with socialism and its egalitarian supporters in America, the word 'liberal' changed meaning, a point on which I have already touched in Chapter 1. It is important to understand this development, since it has entirely transformed both the language and the practice of politics in America and also across the Western world. The classical liberalism of Locke, Montesquieu and Smith was a defence of individual sovereignty against the power of the state, and it promoted limited government, private property, market economics and free associations. In American popular usage today, 'liberalism' means left-liberalism – not to be confused with neo-liberalism, which I discuss in the next chapter – and is expressly contrasted with 'conservatism'. In this usage a liberal is one who leans consciously towards the under-privileged, supports the interests of minorities and socially excluded groups, believes in the use of state power to achieve social justice, and in all probability shares the egalitarian and secular values of the nineteenth-century socialists. The American liberal is certainly not averse to the power of the state, provided it is exerted by liberals, and exerted against conservatives. Anyone who defends the classical liberal position is likely to be regarded, now, as a conservative, on account of the association between classical liberalism and the free market, and the clash between liberal individualism and the dependency culture associated with the welfare state. Readers will be aware of all the intricacies here, and it is best to put them aside, simply acknowledging that, in the battle with socialism, the classical liberal and the conservative now stand side by side.

This helps to explain why Friedrich von Hayek (1899–1993), who expressed his philosophy in *The Constitution of Liberty* (1961), added to that book an appendix entitled 'Why I am not a Conservative', despite the fact that he had become the intellectual hero of the conservative movement with his publication of *The Road to Serfdom* at the end of the Second

World War. Throughout his life Hayek wanted to affirm his identity with the classical liberal tradition, believing that the true cause of the crises leading to two world wars was the steady increase in the power of the state, and its misuse in the pursuit of unobtainable goals. 'Social justice' was the name of one of these goals, and Hayek expressly dismissed the expression as a piece of deceptive Newspeak, used to advance large-scale injustice in the name of its opposite.

Hayek was an economist, student of Eugen von Böhm-Bawerk (1851–1914) and Ludwig von Mises (1881–1973), and like them a prominent member of the Austrian school of economics founded by Carl Menger (1840–1921). But his thought ranged far more widely than economics, and for much of his life, living and teaching in England and America, he saw himself as a social philosopher in the tradition of Locke and Smith. He distanced himself from the conservative movement because he believed that conservative governments, in the aftermath of the Second World War, had simply accepted that civil society should be managed by the state, and as a result had perpetuated the illusions and the policies of the socialists. Despite those reservations it is to Hayek that we owe the most important conservative defence of common-law justice. And like his contemporary Michael Oakeshott (1901–90) he gave a theory of civil society that, properly understood, brings together and revives the insights of both Hegel and Burke.

Hayek's foundational argument is that developed by Mises and other members of the Austrian school during what came to be known as the 'calculation debate' – the debate over the viability of a socialist economy. If a planned economy is to work it must be possible to collect information as to what people want and what they are prepared to give in order to obtain it. Prices in a planned economy must reflect that information: but how can they be calculated a priori, and before people have engaged in the free exchanges which reveal the nature and extent of their desires?

All social action requires information about the wants and needs of indefinitely many people; it also requires spontaneous solutions to conflicts. In a free market the price of a good is determined by the totality of human demands for it, and there can be no better indication of the sacrifice which others are prepared to make in order to obtain a good than the price that attaches to it in a regime of free exchange. The information contained in prices is social, dynamic and practical: it is information concerning what to do in order to satisfy the distant wants of strangers, and it fluctuates in response to changing wants and needs. This information could not exist in a single head, since it is available only in the *process* of exchange, in a society where people are free to buy and sell. Any interference with the market mechanism therefore destroys the information needed in order to make rational economic decisions. Planning, which attempts to reconstruct this information as a static set of data, is invariably irrational since, by fixing the direction and parameters of economic life, it destroys the information on which it depends.

Hayek saw in the calculation argument the possibility to develop a theory of civil society as a whole. The free market is an example of a spontaneous order, which arises by an invisible hand from free association and which generates of its own accord the solutions to economic problems. In like manner, the common law generates a spontaneous legal order, which, because it grows from particular solutions to particular conflicts, inherently tends to restore society to a state of equilibrium – unlike statute law, which tries to anticipate conflicts and thereby creates them. In expounding that idea Hayek noted that law exists in human societies long before anyone conceives the idea of writing it down, and long before the practice of legislation. For law is implied in our free exchanges, which take place under the eye of conscience – Smith's 'impartial spectator'. Hence laws are implied by our conduct, and emerge from free transactions in something like the way the rules of good manners emerge spontaneously in each new sphere of human endeavour – for example the rules of courtesy that arose between drivers on public roads, long before anyone thought to fix them in a 'highway code'.

Hayek sees the economic structure of capitalism, however modified by historical contingencies, as an essential part not only of economic prosperity, but also of the freedom of action to which all social beings aspire. Nevertheless, freedom is durable only when guaranteed by a constitution, and it is no easy matter to develop a constitution that permits liberty while forbidding licence and anarchy. *The Constitution of Liberty* attempts to give an account of the ideal constitution of a modern capitalist state. The result is a mitigated conservatism, in which many of the constitutional devices of the Anglo-American political tradition are upheld as guarantees of stability, which also permit the possibility of reform. Hayek supports democracy in principle, but argues that the mechanisms whereby power is exercised in democracies prevent the emergence of genuine collective choice, and that no political system provides as real an instance of collective choice as that provided by a market. Moreover, whereas in an economic market each individual acts under a budget constraint, under most majority-rule democracies politicians are under no similar constraint, or at least, not immediately: hence the self-regulating conditions of the market cannot easily be achieved in the political sphere.

As his vision widened to include ever more aspects of our social being, Hayek ventured a kind of generalised theory of Smith's 'invisible hand'. He described this as the theory of 'spontaneous order' or 'catallaxy', and expounded it at length in three difficult but rewarding volumes: *Rules and Order* (1973), *The Mirage of Social Justice* (1976) and *The Political Order of a Free People* (1979). The burden of Hayek's argument in these three books is that all attempts to achieve a planned social order, in which goods and opportunities are distributed according to some predetermined formula, will involve removing or impeding the freedom of individuals to make decisions for themselves. Moreover, by removing freedom the plan will inspire resistance, and compel transactions to move beyond its control, into a black market or a private system of justice. Hence the plan will always destroy the possibility of its own implementation – something that has been abundantly illustrated in all communist systems, which produce inequalities in possessions, powers and privileges that far transcend anything to be observed in free economies.

In order to justify itself the socialist plan conscripts every institution and even language to its purpose. For example, it describes the enforced economic equality at which it aims as 'social justice', even though it can be achieved only by the unjust expropriation of assets gained by free agreements. The true meaning of justice, Hayek argues, is that given by Aristotle and followed by Ulpian in the digest of the Roman law – the practice of giving to each person what is due. But the weasel word 'social' sucks out the meaning of 'justice'. Social justice is not a form of justice at all, but a form of moral corruption. It means rewarding people for feckless behaviour, for neglecting their own and their family's well-being, for breaking their agreements and for exploiting their employers.

Hayek's defence of the English common law has been largely overlooked in the literature, but it deserves a mention for two reasons. As an Austrian, brought up under the Roman-law jurisdiction of the Austro-Hungarian Empire, in which law was seen as a system of commands, Hayek might have been tempted to see Parliament as the source of our law and the authority implied in it. Instead he saw the common law as the heart of English society, and the living proof that justice resides in the transactions between freely associating people and not in the plans of a sovereign power. Moreover, Hayek sees the common law as the application of a mode of reasoning that is implicit in those same free transactions. Legal positivists like the English liberal H. L. A. Hart think of common law as 'judge-made' law, as though the law is invented in the courts, and after the facts of the case.[7] No, says Hayek: if it were like that, common-law judgments would always involve an injustice, in judging people according to a law that they could not have known. Common law is judge-*discovered* law. The law encapsulated in the judgment of a case is the one on which the parties already relied, even if without overt and formal knowledge. The law was assumed in their very agreement, and the judge is bringing their shared assumption into the open. Thus in the leading case of *Donoghue* v. *Stevenson* (1932), in which the plaintiff was made ill by a dead snail discovered in the bottle of ginger beer that she was drinking, it was held that a manufacturer of goods for sale is prima facie liable for any harm that is suffered by the one who, in good faith, acquires and makes use of those goods, this being a principle which the contracting parties have implicitly acted upon. Parliament did not have to decide on this rule of law, which has governed product liability ever since, since it was discovered as an assumption in the very conduct that the law was required to regulate.

Hayek's arguments are subtle, far-reaching and directed in a single-minded way against socialism and the philosophy of the plan. His 1944 diatribe, *The Road to Serfdom*, directed against the emerging social democratic consensus at the end of the war, is often picked on for its seeming exaggeration, in suggesting that democratic socialism will move of its own accord towards the totalitarian state. But – like many imperfectly argued books – it had an influence out of all proportion to its intellectual merits, and is still widely accepted as a succinct statement of the anti-socialist case.

7   H. L. A. Hart, *The Concept of Law*, Oxford, 1961.

Less influential, but in their way more true to reality, were the post-war articles published as a book in 1962 by Michael Oakeshott: *Rationalism and Politics*. In these powerfully written essays Oakeshott points to the damage done when politics is directed from above towards a goal – whether liberty, equality or fraternity – and where all policies and negotiations are formulated by reference to that goal. By 'rationalism' Oakeshott means the attempt to see political association in 'means-ends' terms, the end being clearly formulated, and the means justified in terms of it. The result is inevitably the destruction of compromise and free association, and the imposition of an order that no one subject to it would have consented to. Like Hayek, Oakeshott is reviving and amplifying the original insights of Smith and Burke, showing that reasonable policies are not necessarily 'rational', since they emerge from the unpredictable amalgamation of our choices, and without the adoption of a common goal.

Oakeshott followed this argument with an attack on 'ideology'. This was his name for political belief systems – collections of ideas, goals and theories designed to justify the believer in taking charge of the future. The Marxist theory of revolution, the fascist idea of the corporate state under quasi-military command, the Nazi philosophy of race were all ideologies in Oakeshott's sense. They were designed to justify political control, by creating, at the intellectual level, a sense of emergency: only if *we* do *this* and do it *now* will the future of society be secured. Against ideology Oakeshott advocated a politics of 'intimations' – intuitive understandings of how things are and how they might be changed, which arise from an active engagement in the political order and an openness to conversation with others. The aims of political association, Oakeshott insisted, are not imposed but discovered, and this means that politics is an art of listening and enquiring, rather than barking out orders or reading from a sheet of a priori rules.

Ideology proposes a kind of politics of war: the message is, you are either with us or against us, and we shall win in any case. This goes counter to the entire political tradition of Anglo-American representative government, which involves the acceptance of certain procedures and institutions as 'given' – i.e. as creating the framework within which disagreements can be negotiated. Such a form of government should not be understood as a means to an end, or a solution to a problem, but as a way in which people live together in mutual understanding. It is both the end and the means, the solution and the problem.

In his mature work, *On Human Conduct* (1975), Oakeshott developed an elusive but influential theory of 'civil association', the term he used to announce a particular conception of civil society. He wished to contrast this conception with the socialist and left-liberal theories that, consciously or not, saw civil society as subservient to, and conscripted by, the state. Oakeshott draws a contrast between civil association and 'enterprise association'. An enterprise association has a purpose, an over-arching goal (whether commercial, military or political), which defines an agenda for the association as a whole. Civil association is not founded in a contract, nor is it devoted to a purpose. It should be construed rather on the model of a conversation, in which purposes, meanings and information emerge unpredictably from the friendly interchange of the participants. Oakeshott's frequent references to conversation suggest that this is, for him, a kind of paradigm of an association that is to be treated as an 'end in itself'. In a way the argument can be seen as a return to an idea that we find in Aristotle, who believed that friendship is the ultimate foundation of legitimacy in the city-state. For Aristotle friendship is an indisputable good, one that requires no further purpose to justify it, though one that admits of many kinds and many degrees. The highest friendship, for which virtue is a qualification and a result, is mimicked by a society of citizens, who strive, through emulation and example, to honour each other as friends, and to enjoy the benefits that come from friendship precisely because they do not officiously pursue them.

Oakeshott was less interested in targeting the totalitarian movements of the twentieth century than in mounting an assault on the dirigisme that had entered British politics as a kind of consensus movement after the war. It was for several decades assumed that the state had the right and the duty to 'manage', not only the economy, but the education system, the relief of poverty, the pattern of settlements and the industries that furnish them with labour, the terms and conditions of employment – in short, just about anything on which the well-being and security of the people might seem to depend. Throughout his life Oakeshott's concern was to show that this kind of politics involves a profound mistake about the nature of civil society, and a blindness to those aspects of the human condition – conversation, friendship, sport, poetry and the arts – in which our minds are turned towards things of intrinsic value, and away from getting and spending. It is noteworthy that religion occurs only as an afterthought to Oakeshott's reflections on civil association. This is indicative of the radical secularisation of English conservatism in the post-war period, a secularisation that is equally apparent in Austrian conservatism in the wake of the First World War. World wars tend to leave religion in general, and Christianity in particular, in a condition of radical self-doubt.

Oakeshott's position as a professor of political philosophy at the London School of Economics enabled him to build up a network of sympathetic students and colleagues and for a while the LSE politics department became a centre of conservative resistance to the prevailing socialist consensus (see the next chapter). The elusiveness of Oakeshott's theories, and his preference to hint at his beliefs rather than to make them explicit, have been regretted by his followers. And like so many conservatives, he refused to endorse the political movement and the party that wore the conservative badge. Like F. R. Leavis, he was non-committal towards religion, and did not see either Christianity or the Anglican Church as having any precise role to play in the kind of civil association that he wished for. His view of civil association was, in the end, elitist, tailored to his own experience as a don and a sceptical intellectual, and connected only at the margins with the social, cultural and political battles of the day.

The confrontation with socialism took a slightly different form in America. Until the New Deal (1933–7) of

President Roosevelt, the idea that the state could manage the economy, engage in business enterprises of its own, and take proper charge of the health and welfare of the citizens was regarded by many Americans as an aberration, characteristic of European socialism but hardly compatible with the American Constitution. By degrees, however, socialist ideas began to penetrate American intellectual and political life, and the conservative response to them was to a large extent triggered by the Great Depression, the plight of the new urban working class, and the resulting sympathy among intellectuals for communism. The history of this response is complex, and embroiled in controversies surrounding the New Deal, and stories of Soviet infiltration and espionage. For present purposes it must suffice to consider two representative figures, both of whom began as communist sympathisers, and one of whom was for a while a Soviet spy: James Burnham (1905–87), and Whittaker Chambers (1901–61).

James Burnham was a sociologist, profoundly influenced by the Marxist analysis of capitalist society. He at first sympathised with the communist call for a new social order, in which the crises and hardships of capitalism would be overcome and class divisions brought to an end. He helped to organise the American Workers Party in 1933, and to turn it in a direction favoured by Trotsky, with whom he formed a friendship by correspondence. The ruthlessness of Stalin, however, the Soviet invasions of the Baltic States and Finland, and finally the Nazi–Soviet Pact, opened his eyes to the reality of communism, and to the destructive effect of the Marxist theories that had inspired it. He saw the effect of these theories also in the New Deal, and set out to defend American capitalism from 'New Dealism', as he called it, which he regarded as an assault on the American liberal tradition. It was a mark of Burnham's Marxist formation that the term 'capitalism' constantly occurred to him as the name of his cause. But, as the years went by, he became more and more obviously a conservative, and influential as such.

The movement in that direction began with *The Managerial Revolution* (1941), in which Burnham accused socialism of the faults that the Marxists had attributed to capitalism. In all its forms, Burnham argued, the tendency of socialism is not to produce a classless society as promised but on the contrary to generate a new and intransigent ruling class of bureaucrats – the managerial elite. This class would automatically demand a planned economy, restrictions on creativity and enterprise and the encroachment on property rights. Burnham criticised New Dealism in similar terms, arguing that it prepared the American people for the managerial takeover, and blinded them to what was really at stake in the confrontation with communism. In *The Struggle for the World* (1947), he laid out a battle plan for what was to be known as the cold war, arguing for shared citizenship between America and Great Britain, and a unity of all relevant forces against the communist threat.

Finally, in *Suicide of the West* (1964), he provided conservatives with the language and vision with which to define both the confrontation with communism and the ineffectiveness of the Western powers in dealing with it. In this book Burnham moves towards cultural conservatism, defending the moral and religious heritage of the West, and denouncing 'that jellyfish brand of contemporary liberalism – pious, guilt-ridden, do-goody – which uses the curious dogma of "some truth on both sides" as its principal sales line.' In many ways it was due to Burnham's incisive mind, trained in Marxist debunking, and used to seeing through all ideas to the powers that advance behind them, that American conservatism began to pit itself against the newly re-defined 'liberalism', conceived as an all-comprehending state of mind. Liberals, as portrayed by Burnham, are in a state of guilt about their privileges, unable to affirm the good things that surround and protect them, and wishing to excuse every fault in their enemies by naming some fault of their own. Rather than face up to the reality of Soviet tyranny they play the game of 'moral equivalence', placing the faults of American democracy side by side with those of totalitarian communism and implying that neither can be judged without equally condemning the other.

Burnham was called on to head the psychological warfare unit of what was to become the CIA, and helped to set up the Congress of Cultural Freedom in 1950, which used CIA money to sponsor publications that would impede the leftist takeover of the culture in America and Europe. This work, which turned Burnham increasingly towards a kind of cultural conservatism, led to his being effectively cast out from the intellectual community when the principal funder of the Congress was eventually exposed. Like many of those ex-radicals who changed sides in the wake of the Soviet crimes, he was marginalised by those whom he sought to convert.

The same fate awaited Whittaker Chambers, the communist sympathiser who belonged to a circle of spies in the administration of President Roosevelt, and who, awakened by this experience to the nature of communism, left the Party and its network, eventually betraying his fellow agents to the US government. Chambers was a complex and tortured character and also a public figure, a brilliant writer who rose to become a senior editor of *Time* magazine. But his appearances in court in the various espionage trials in which he was involved were used by the leftist networks to discredit him, and it was not until the publication of *Witness* (1952), telling the whole story of his communist involvement, that he became a central figure in the conservative movement.

*Witness* is not simply a factual account of the Soviet espionage network in Washington, and the damage done by that network during and after the war. It is a penetrating psychological study of the mental slavery and moral degradation upon which the communist system depends. Chambers describes the negativity of the communist vision in unforgettable terms, emphasising the machine-like nature of its betrayals, murders and genocides. The Soviet spy as described by Chambers is not an enterprising hero, exposing himself to danger for a noble cause, but a kind of bureaucrat, receiving and passing on death sentences written beneath an all-excusing rubber stamp.

Several European intellectuals were at the time writing of communism in similar terms – notably George Orwell, Arthur Koestler and Czesław Miłosz. But the influence of *Witness* was the greater on account of being a story from the inside. It described communism as a disease within the State Department, which had also been a disease in Chambers's own soul – the soul of an American who, in rescuing himself, had rediscovered both his religious faith and his identity with the spiritual culture of his homeland. Henceforth anti-communism was viewed by conservatives in America as part of their self-definition, a kind of proof of their spiritual purity. Although McCarthyism to some extent discredited anti-communism in the public perception, Chambers was able to present it in another way, as a kind of revelation of American culture. Communism, as Chambers described it, is a systematic negation of the soul of America, something to be resisted not merely with outward force, but with inward devotion to the American idea, which is as much a spiritual as a political inheritance.

The challenge of communism had come early to continental Europe, where the short-lived Paris Commune of 1871 had made communism seem both possible to its supporters and seriously frightening to its opponents. The intellectual reaction in central Europe is typified by the arguments of Hayek, discussed above. But in France and the Mediterranean countries, where Marxist, futurist and radical utopian ideas swept across the intellectual landscape in the early twentieth century, the threat of total disruption gave rise once again to a religious rejection, as with Maistre and Chateaubriand, of the leftist world view.

The twentieth-century version of French conservatism is therefore associated with the *renouveau catholique*, which was in part a reaction to the French defeat in the Franco-Prussian war, and in part a response to a long spell of secular materialism, republican government, and modernising projects inspired by the rivalry with Germany and England. The leading light of this Catholic renewal was the poet Charles Péguy (1873–1914), whose journal *Cahiers de la Quinzaine* carried some of the most important writers from the turn of the century. Péguy had socialist leanings in politics; but he also envisaged a new kind of French patriotism, centred not on the Republic or the Revolution, but on the figure of Jeanne d'Arc, the brave peasant girl who had served her king, her faith and her country, and whose martyrdom by the English had established her as spiritual symbol and patron saint of France. It was thanks in great part to Péguy (and in particular to his strange and evocative poem, *Le mystère de la charité de Jeanne d'Arc*) that Jeanne was canonised in 1920.

Following the First World War French intellectual life was polarised between the Catholic revival and the increasingly Marxist movement on the left. The conflict was fought out in works of philosophy as well as in art, music and literature, and the conservative side was never embodied in a political party or even in a coherent political movement. There was an agrarian component, associated with the novelist Jean Giono (1895–1970) and the philosopher Gustave Thibon (1903–2001), as well as a directly theological component, associated with the philosopher Jacques Maritain (1882–1973) and his poetic wife Raïssa (1883–1960).

The movement that grew from these inputs was not a political programme but a bid for the soul of France, and its main partisans would have regarded the arguments of Hayek or Oakeshott as quaint speculations, of no significance in the real life of the mind. The real expressions of conservative sentiment were to be found in the Christ paintings of Georges Rouault (1871–1958), in the novels of François Mauriac (1885–1970) describing a devout provincial way of life, and in the music of Francis Poulenc (1899–1963), whose late opera, *Dialogues des Carmélites* (1957), based on a screenplay by the Catholic novelist Georges Bernanos, is not only a moving work of art in itself, but a kind of 'taking back' of the French Revolution. In this ferment of creative energy ideas were put to the test in works of the imagination and seldom if ever entertained as philosophical arguments – one reason, it seems to me, why French conservatism has always been so difficult to define, and impossible to separate from the thought of France as a spiritual condition and a consecrated place.

One writer, however, merits special attention from the student of intellectual conservatism, and that is the philosopher and mystic Simone Weil (1909–43), whose posthumous work *L'enracinement* (*The Need for Roots*, 1949) contains a kind of digest of cultural conservatism, conceived as a state of mind rather than a political programme. Weil was, like so many of her contemporaries, a product of leftist and Marxist ways of thinking, who moved suddenly in another direction, prior to the Second World War. Weil was of Jewish descent, and had been brought up in a secular and atheist household. However, she had always been drawn to Christianity, influenced in this by her friend and mentor Gustave Thibon.

Following a beatific call in the Church of Santa Maria degli Angeli in Assisi in 1935, and a reading of George Herbert's poetry, Weil accepted the Christian faith (though not baptism) and also, along with it, her commitment to France. She hoped to be a martyr to both causes, in the manner of Jeanne d'Arc, and was for a while accepted for training as an agent in the French Resistance by the British Special Operations Executive, she being resident in wartime England as a refugee from Nazism. However, failing health prevented this, and Weil poured out in her writings the passionate call to sacrifice that she addressed to herself and had wished to live by.

Weil's mystical Christianity, and identification with the victims of both totalitarian politics and unbridled industrialism, compelled highly influential, if eccentric, reflections on the state of contemporary society, together with proposals for its political revitalisation. She identified the chief evil of modern civilisation as *déracinement*, and attempted to analyse the *enracinement* (putting down of roots) that had protected humanity in the past, and might again protect it in the future, from social corrosion. This aspect of her thought was influenced by the agrarian conservatism of Thibon and Giono. Human beings have roots, Weil argued, by virtue of their active participation in a collective, which conserves in living form a social and spiritual inheritance, and which continues to offer presentiments of a shared future. That idea – which is a core teaching of cultural conservatism in all its forms – was expressed in poetic and mystical prose that profoundly affected her intellectual followers, including T. S. Eliot, Albert Camus, and Popes Paul VI and John Paul II.

Weil attempted to reconcile her emphasis on particularised attachments with a universalist morality, derived from Kant, and also with a respect for hierarchy, diversity, private property and territory. She defended true patriotism (a local intimation of world citizenship) against nationalism (a form of *déracinement* comparable in its effects to the corrosiveness of industrial production, of which she was a trenchant critic). She claimed both Christian and Marxist inspiration for her rejection of the effects of industrialisation, and proposed utopian schemes for the amelioration of the condition of labour, by preventing the emergence of large-scale industry. Like Ruskin, she wished labour to be an exercise in willing obedience, founded in allegiance to others and to the social order – a form of pious attachment to life in which gravity and grace would attach to all daily actions. (*Gravity and Grace*, edited from Weil's notebooks by Thibon, was published in 1952.) Weil's profoundly moral view of economic life influenced also her idea of law, which she thought (with Kant) could enforce morality without infringing freedom. She admired the English constitution as a seeming expression of that idea, though her profound individualism caused her to hold that law is not enough, and that salvation comes only through the inward resolve to sacrifice.

Weil's cultural conservatism has been echoed elsewhere in Europe, and I conclude this chapter with a brief glance at one of the last intellectual conservatives from Spain, the philosopher José Ortega y Gasset (1883–1955) who, like Weil, addressed the spiritual condition of our civilisation, and sought the inner remedy to its decadence. Ortega was a professor of philosophy who developed his own system, inspired in part by the phenomenology of Edmund Husserl

(1859–1938). But his main contribution to conservatism consists in books addressed to the reading public, in which all philosophical technicalities are laid aside and a lucid, evocative prose is put to the service of moral and political teaching. Three works reveal in their titles the direction of his thought: *España invertebrada* (*Invertebrate Spain*, 1921), *La deshumanización del arte* (*The Dehumanisation of Art*, 1925) and (the most famous) *La rebelión de las masas* (*The Revolt of the Masses*, 1930).

Ortega was briefly a member of parliament in the Republican government, but left Spain at the outbreak of the civil war. His writings, prior to that time, were based in a profound love of, and respect for, the national culture of Spain. The settled way of life, under the protection of the Catholic Church, but in full recognition of the material realities of a peasant economy, brought with it certain virtues which had marked the Spanish character and which would always be needed if the country were to exist as an independent republic. These virtues – courage, fidelity, and a hardened self-reliance – went with a popular culture that emphasised the unity of the family and the sanctity of rites of passage. Ortega's traditional and 'vertebrate' Spain involved an emphasis on sexual difference, the masculine and the feminine being publicly put to the test, as in bullfighting, flamenco dancing and the blood feuds of rural communities. Ortega wrote evocatively of the matador culture and English-style hunting in *La caza y los toros* (*Hunting and Bulls*, 1960), evoking the same tragic rootedness that is expressed in the poems of Federico García Lorca, who was, however, a man of the left, and one of the victims of fascism in the civil war.

In *The Revolt of the Masses* (1930), Ortega expresses a certain aristocratic disdain for the destructive activities of people no longer obedient to traditional moral and social order, and argues that the 'masses' exist because a new form of political organisation has made them possible. He identifies this as the modern kind of democracy, in which individuals are regarded as having equal rights regardless of power, and all privilege is treated with hostility and, where possible, undermined, so as to restore the uniformity of the whole. The book, like Tocqueville's *Democracy in America*, is a survey of what democracy and the idea of equal citizenship will in the long run imply, and a plea to retain those elements of the old culture that will form a line of resistance to the emerging mediocrity.

Ortega's Spain was swept away by the civil war, as the rest of continental Europe was destroyed by Nazism, fascism and communism. Not much remains of the society whose virtues Ortega lamented, just as not much remains of the Anglican peace evoked by Eliot or the *enracinement* defended by Thibon and Weil. Nevertheless, cultural conservatism remains a significant intellectual movement, and is one part of the complex posture to the world that is conservatism today. In the final chapter I will attempt to summarise that posture, focusing as before on Britain and America.

# 6

## CONSERVATISM NOW

Modern conservatism began as a defence of tradition against the calls for popular sovereignty; it became an appeal on behalf of religion and high culture against the materialist doctrine of progress, before joining forces with the classical liberals in the fight against socialism. In its most recent attempt to define itself it has become the champion of Western civilisation against its enemies, and against two of those enemies in particular: political correctness (notably its constraints on freedom of expression and its emphasis in everything on Western guilt) and religious extremism, especially the militant Islamism promoted by the Wahhabi–Salafi sects. In all these transformations something has remained the same, namely the conviction that good things are more easily destroyed than created, and the determination to hold on to those good things in the face of politically engineered change.

British intellectual conservatism since the Second World War has existed only as a fragmentary force on the edge of intellectual life, with little or no connection to politics, and with virtually no support in the universities. John Stuart Mill's dismissal of the Tories as 'the stupid party' expresses a view that has remained orthodox among intellectuals, and even those who have most clearly understood and defended the conservative message have been reluctant to confess to the label. Particularly significant in this connection is George Orwell (Eric Blair) (1903–50), who described himself as a socialist and a partisan of the working class, while dissociating himself completely from the left intellectuals with their 'smelly little orthodoxies', and their refusal, in the great crisis of the twentieth century, to respond to the call of patriotic duty.

Orwell's novel *Nineteen Eighty-Four* (1949) is well known for its description of an imaginary form of totalitarianism, adding certain words to political language that have proved irreplaceable. These words satirise the acronyms of Bolshevism ('Cominform', 'Comintern', 'Proletkult', etc.) and include *Newspeak* (designed to meet the ideological needs of *Ingsoc*, or English socialism, and to make heretical thought – *thoughtcrime* – impossible); *prolefeed* (rubbishy entertainment and fictitious news for the masses, or *proles*); *unperson* (one who has been carefully removed from history); and *doublethink*: 'the power of holding two contradictory propositions in one's mind simultaneously, and accepting both of them'. Orwell also invented the 'thought police', as the last word in despotic efficiency, and wrote, in *Animal Farm* (1945), the most famous of all satires of communism, which he epitomised in the phrase 'all animals are equal, but some are more equal than others'.

In effect, Orwell's political fables contain an accurate and penetrating prophecy of the political correctness that has since invaded intellectual life in both Britain and America. The humourless and relentless policing of language, so as to prevent heretical thoughts from arising, the violence done to traditional categories and natural ways of describing things, the obliteration of memory and assiduous policing of the past – all these things, so disturbingly described in *Nineteen Eighty-Four*, are now routinely to be observed on university campuses on both sides of the Atlantic, and those conservatives who draw attention to the phenomenon, as Allan Bloom did in his influential book *The Closing of the American Mind* (1987), are frequently marginalised or even demonised as representatives of one of the forbidden 'isms' or 'phobias' of the day – racism, sexism, homophobia, transphobia, Islamophobia, etc. In a society devoted to 'inclusion' the only 'phobia' permitted is that of which conservatives are the target.

This situation, which puts conservatives at an enormous disadvantage in the intellectual world, has inevitably changed their way of defining themselves, and made the 'culture wars' central to their sense of what they are fighting for and why. Understanding political correctness and finding the ways to combat it have therefore become prominent among conservative causes. Is political correctness simply the final stage of liberal individualism – the stage at which all barriers to a self-chosen identity are to be removed? If so, which of those barriers can conservatives still defend against the onslaught, and how can they justify the attempt? Or is it rather a derogation from the great liberal tradition, a way in which equality has become so urgent and dominating a cause that nothing of liberty remains, and all social life is absorbed into a relentless witch-hunt against the defenders of social distinctions?

Orwell's essays, notably 'The Lion and the Unicorn: Socialism and the English Genius' (1941), are classics of cultural conservatism, which find Weil's *enracinement* in the small-scale work and unassuming customs of the urban working class. Although in no way tempted by Christianity, the doctrine of which he felt had little appeal to the English, Orwell believed that the English working class was imbued with a Christian spirit, undemonstrative and straightforwardly compassionate, and he saw this reflected in all the habits and rituals that helped them survive the great hardships of the war.

Orwell owed his standing among post-war intellectuals to his self-identification as a man of the left. Few at the time were prepared to admit to being conservative and, as mentioned in the last chapter, Hayek, the most powerful intellect on the right, preferred to describe himself as a liberal. (Incidentally, Orwell published a largely favourable review of Hayek's *The Road to Serfdom* in *The Observer*, on 4 April 1944.) Nevertheless, there was and is a real conservative intellectual class in modern Britain. The conservative movement succeeded in putting down roots here and there in the academic world, and in particular in the department of government in the LSE under Michael Oakeshott. The circle in and around that department included the Iraqi Jew, Elie Kedourie, whose staunch defence of the Tory tradition in foreign policy against what he saw as the creeping culture of liberal guilt (*The Chatham House Version, and Other Middle Eastern Studies*, 1970) sent a powerful message to those who had not yet lost their faith in the patriotic ideals and national sovereignty of Great Britain. Kedourie was a staunch critic of 'ideological nationalism' of the kind that had swept across Europe in the nineteenth century and which was, in his view, a threat to law and order all across the modern world (*Nationalism in Asia and Africa*, 1970). But he saw patriotism of the British kind as the phlegmatic opposite of the crowd emotions that had been stirred by modern mass politics.

Another LSE-based exile, the Hungarian-born Peter Bauer (1915–2002), mounted in a series of publications the conservative case against foreign aid – the practice, as he put it, of 'rewarding governments for the impoverishment of their people' (*Dissent on Development*, 1972). And yet another LSE don, Kenneth Minogue (1930–2013), an immigrant from New Zealand, devoted his life to the intellectual defence of the English inheritance and the unwritten constitution of liberty. In his later writings (*The Servile Mind. How Democracy Erodes the Moral Life*, 2010) Minogue gave sharp expression to the anti-democratic tendency in conservatism, a tendency that I have already noted in Ortega. Minogue argued that the proliferation of democratic values will always, in the end, undermine the culture of distinction and emulation on which a lasting civil society depends. His was one of several attacks on the welfare system inspired by the work of the American social scientist Charles Murray (*Losing Ground: American Social Policy 1950–1980*, 1984).

It is perhaps no accident that recent British conservatism has included so many immigrant voices. For it is the privilege of the immigré to speak without irony of the British Empire and of the unique culture, institutions and laws that have made Britain the safe place of refuge for so many in a smouldering world. Natives are more reluctant to speak out, for fear of the political correctness that sees conservatism, in all its forms, as the enemy. Not censorship only but a culture of repudiation reigns in the media and the universities, and to become known as someone who speaks out for the institutions and hierarchies of Old England is to court ridicule and ostracism from the left establishment.

Nevertheless, cells of dissidents existed, and their influence has been out of proportion to their size. Typical of the phenomenon is the school of historians that arose around Maurice Cowling (1926–2005), in the Cambridge College of Peterhouse. Without exaggerating the importance of Cowling, I shall quote here from the obituary that I published on the site of *Open Democracy* in 2005, since it gives some of the flavour of the flamboyant dissident culture that has flourished in a few redoubts during my lifetime:

> Maurice's intellect was an immense negative force, which could undermine any conviction and pour scorn on any emotional attachment. He regarded conservative beliefs in the same light as he regarded all beliefs other than those of the Christian faith – as self-serving expedients, whereby individuals sought the good opinion of their fellows and closed their minds to uncomfortable realities. He himself lived with uncomfortable realities on easy-going terms, demanding only intelligent pupils, the company of seedy journalists and a supply of whisky in order to continue impishly smiling at the unremitting spectacle of human folly.
>
> Maurice's iconoclastic approach to the world of ideas was in part inspired by his forays into the world of journalism. These culminated in 1971, when his life-long friend George Gale, being appointed editor of *The Spectator*, invited Maurice to edit the book pages. Under the guidance of Gale and Cowling *The Spectator* became a serious vehicle of ideas,

and an articulate conservative voice. The venture came to a premature end when *The Spectator* changed hands in 1974. Maurice returned to his rooms in Peterhouse, to continue work on his magnum opus, *Religion and Public Doctrine in Modern England*, the third and longest volume of which appeared in 2001. The purpose of this work was twofold: first to show the commanding influence of ideas on the development of modern British society, and secondly to point to the enduring relevance of religion in determining just what those ideas have amounted to.

Maurice's method was the very opposite of that advocated by the *Annales* school of historiography. Parish registers, hospital statistics, demographic trends and socio-economic surveys had little significance, in his writing, in comparison with pamphlets by obscure Anglican clergymen, exchanges of letters between members of the House of Lords, and the quarrels and crises of Oxbridge dons. The argument over Anglicanism that began with Keble and the Oxford movement [an early manifestation of cultural conservatism] was carried over, in Maurice's view, into all the subsequent intellectual movements that affected the course of English history: the partisanship of culture against science in Coleridge, Arnold, Ruskin and Leavis; the debates over the constitution in Mill, Acton, Dicey and Maitland; the conflict between liberalism and conservatism in Parliament and out of it; the whole tendency of modern English culture as the chill winds of secularism swept across it and a sense of the fragility and uniqueness of England replaced the old religious certainty of the Book of Common Prayer.

Maurice's critics regarded his choice of topics as eccentric and his historical method as unfounded. Others, however, have found inspiration and illumination in his meticulous attention to the mental and spiritual makeup of public figures. If ideas are as important as he makes them out to be, then a life spent like Maurice's, in examining, mocking and refuting them, has not been spent in vain. And the immense breadth of his learning meant that everything he wrote brings new information and a new perspective on its subject. He was a trenchant critic of liberalism, and his book on Mill was the first major attempt since that of Sir James Fitzjames Stephen (*Liberty, Equality, Fraternity*, 1873–4) to identify Mill's liberal outlook as a threat to ordinary human decencies. But, while Maurice inoculated several generations of undergraduates against liberal orthodoxy, his own positive opinions were hard to discern through the smokescreen of irony.

The irony that I felt to be central to Maurice Cowling's world view was, in fact, a distinguishing feature of British, and specifically English, conservatism in recent times. Conservative commentators, in their attempt to rise above the censoriousness of their critics, would simultaneously express their views and ironically withdraw from them, as though not wishing to be accused of the naïve habit of believing in what could no longer be accepted as the literal truth. This was especially true of the group of sceptical writers around *The Spectator* and *The Daily Telegraph*, who met and drank in the Kings and Keys pub in Fleet Street (above which, at the time, the *Telegraph* was edited), and in the nearby wine bar El Vino, which served both the journalists and the lawyers of the inns of court. These writers included T. E. Utley, the blind leader-writer of the *Telegraph* who did much to shape the intellectual agenda of Margaret Thatcher's governments, the journalists Colin Welch and Sir Peregrine Worsthorne, the novelist Kingsley Amis and the historian Paul Johnson, a defector from the left whose

comprehensive vision of world history has been an important resource for those who see the defence of Western civilisation as the true conservative cause.

Johnson belongs to another category of British dissident – the class of freelance historians, who break free from
the constraints of academic history and devote themselves
to the big questions of modern government. The younger
generation of British conservatives contains many such
historians, including Andrew Roberts, Niall Ferguson and
Jane Ridley. And many of them, like Maurice Cowling,
draw inspiration from one of the great English thinkers of
the nineteenth century, F. W. Maitland (1850–1906), who,
in his posthumously published lectures, *The Constitutional
History of England* (1908), gave the classic proof that the
constitution of the UK is a definite entity, even though tacit
and procedural, to be deduced from custom rather than
from any written document.

Maitland initiated a century-long attempt to reclaim
English history for the conservative cause, by arguing
that it is not the Enlightenment that had made individual
liberty into the foundation of our political order, but the
common law and parliamentary representation. Maitland
argued that limited government had been the rule rather
than the exception in England, that the rights claimed by
seventeenth- and eighteenth-century theorists had always
been implied in the common law, and that the process of
political conciliation had been the principal organ of constitutional change from medieval times. The Marxist theory
of history, which sees these things as developing in response
to economic forces, rather than to innate principles of their

own, does not easily survive Maitland's detailed account of English constitutional history.

Maitland also developed a theory of corporate personality, inspired partly by the German conservative jurist Otto von Gierke (1841–1921) and partly by the English law. He emphasised equity and the law of trusts as singular achievements of the English genius – ways in which people combined for a common purpose without threat to, or permission from, the state. Those institutions caused the early emergence in England of a society in which free association and autonomous institutions limited the powers of central government. In the end it has been Maitland's vision of English uniqueness that has been the inspiration for British conservatism in our time, and the real reason why it is historians, rather than economists or philosophers, who have adapted that vision to the needs of the moment.

American intellectual conservatism has followed a slightly different trajectory. Notwithstanding its liberal constitution, the United States of America is in many ways the place where conservatism, as a social and political philosophy, has been most influential, both in the intellectual life of the nation and in the practice of government. It is also a place where you can confess to being a conservative without being socially ostracised.

There are two main reasons for this. The first is that the Constitution was designed as a *federal* constitution, whose purpose was to unite the States while imposing the minimum number of conditions on the diverse people of the Union. A great many matters pertinent to the government of modern communities were left to the individual state legislatures, and it is in the attempt to recapture powers from the federal constitution, so as to maintain existing customs and traditions, that conservative sentiment has been most forceful.

The second reason is connected, namely that many of the institutions and customs on which American society depends are the product of civil association and not governed either by federal bodies or by the legal structures of the states. Throughout its growth as a modern nation America has been built from below, through the free association of its citizens – a point noted and praised by Tocqueville in *Democracy in America*. This has offered scope for conservatism as a philosophy of civil society – a philosophy that outlines and justifies the intrinsic forms of civil order, against the attempt to control and amend them through the institutions of the state.

Both libertarians and conservatives in America emphasise the need to free society from the grip of the state. But while the libertarian argues that political thought and practice should refrain from requiring any kind of conformity to law or principle other than the bare minimum necessary for the maintenance of individual freedom, the conservative believes – for the reasons just hinted at – that there is something more at stake. Society depends for its health and continuity on customs and traditions that are at risk from individual freedom, even if they are also expressions of it. The philosophical burden of American conservatism has been to define those customs and traditions and to show how they might endure and flourish from their own inner dynamic, outside the control of the state.

One effect of the American genius for civil association is of particular importance in this connection: the liberal arts college. This has created an extensive system of higher education, in which schools can choose their curriculum, their values and their aims without reference to political factors and, if necessary, in defiance of political correctness. And the vastness of America, its great wealth and opportunities, mean that other such initiatives are always occurring and new things are always growing, so that the conservative virus, notwithstanding the most vigorous fumigation from the left, will always be taking root again in some dank and life-infested corner. It is impossible in the space of this chapter to mention all relevant personalities, but two in particular will serve as illustrations: William F. Buckley and Russell Kirk.

William F. Buckley Jr (1925–2008) has been described by George H. Nash as, for his generation, 'the pre-eminent voice of American conservatism, and its first great ecumenical figure',[8] 'ecumenical' because Buckley attempted to synthesise in his writings and his life the three principal aspects of the American conservative movement: cultural conservatism, economic liberalism and anti-communism. Buckley's first book, the highly influential *God and Man at Yale* (1951), set the tone for his life and work, in attacking the university that he attended for its blatantly atheist, and incipiently anti-American, culture. From the beginning Buckley, a devout Roman Catholic, was a dissident, a witty critic of establishments, and an evangelist for lost causes. In 1955 he established *National Review*, which became and

8  National Review Online, 28 February 2008.

remains the most convinced and convincing of the many conservative journals that have arisen in America since the war. Through the pages of the *Review*, through his many books and articles, and his TV series of interviews, *Firing Line*, Buckley tirelessly sought to define conservatism as a political movement, in which ideas have a leading role, and the religious and social heritage of America finds a voice adapted to the times.

Buckley's defence of economic liberalism put him in the same camp as the radical individualist, Ayn Rand (1905–82), whose philosophy has influenced several generations of Americans, being expressly presented as an aggressive response to communism and a defence of the entrepreneurial culture of America. Influenced equally by Nietzsche and Darwin, Rand saw in capitalism the mechanism whereby societies create the elites needed to govern them, by hardening both will and wit in the flame of competition. She described her philosophy as 'objectivism', believing that it shows people as they are, rather than as we should, in our sentimental moments, like them to be. She believed that her vision had the backing of science and was as dismissive of religion as the Marxists against whom she waged her lifelong intellectual battle.

Rand argued that it is a mere illusion to believe that the poorer specimens of mankind will benefit from socialism, since socialist policies merely prevent the best and most useful people from exercising their skills and talents. But we all depend upon the success of these people, who create the material and moral space in which lesser beings can find their niche (*The Virtue of Selfishness*, 1964). In her novels,

Rand several times attempted to paint the portrait of the Nietzschean Übermensch, and, although the result does not appeal to everyone, it clearly appealed to her many followers, whose fervent support ensured that she became one of the most successful writers of her time, and one prepared ostentatiously to live the life of the Übermensch herself.

Buckley was one of those to whom Rand did not appeal. He found her atheism repugnant, and her peculiar brand of radical individualism, detached from all traditions and all normal forms of accommodation with human weakness and imperfection, completely alien to what he saw as the essential kindness of the American inheritance. It was important, he believed, to detach American conservatism from Rand's Nietzschean supremacism, which was an alien import, imbued with the exorbitant spirit of the Russian Revolution, from the aftermath of which Rand herself had fled into American exile. In 1964, he wrote of 'her desiccated philosophy's conclusive incompatibility with the conservative's emphasis on transcendence, intellectual and moral,' as well as 'the incongruity of tone, that hard, schematic, implacable, unyielding, dogmatism that is in itself intrinsically objectionable, whether it comes from the mouth of Ehrenburg, Savonarola or Ayn Rand.'[9]

In a similar way Buckley used the pages of the *National Review* to distance conservatism from anti-Semitism, and from any other kind of racial stereotyping. The important goal, for him, was to establish a believable stance towards

9   William F. Buckley Jr, 'Notes toward an Empirical Definition of Conservatism,' in *What is Conservatism?*, edited by Frank S. Meyer, 1964, p. 214

the modern world, in which all Americans, whatever their race or background, could be included, and which would uphold the religious and social traditions of the American people, as well as the institutions of government as the Founders had conceived them. He came to admire Martin Luther King, and believed that conservatives had made a great error in opposing the civil rights movement in the 1960s.

Buckley engaged actively in the 'culture wars', with a twice-weekly column, *On the Right*, syndicated to 320 newspapers across America. He saw in the 1964 presidential candidate, Barry Goldwater, the hope for a revitalisation of the American way of life, with religion, family and Constitution restored to their central place in the affections of the people, and the country taking a firm stance against the communist and socialist threat both at home and abroad. Ayn Rand was also, at the time, an ardent supporter of Goldwater, who captured the imagination of many intellectual dissidents, at the moment when America was wobbling towards a soft kind of quasi-socialism. Goldwater's defeat and disappearance from the political scene fundamentally changed the emphasis of American conservatism, which has been fighting rear-guard actions ever since.

One of those rear-guard actions concerns the Constitution and the role of the Supreme Court in defining it. In a series of judgments, egged on by campus liberals such as Ronald Dworkin, and responding to cultural shifts which go well beyond the universities in their reach, the Supreme Court has acquired the habit of reading into the Constitution rights and freedoms that would never have occurred to the Founding Fathers, or which would have been regarded by them with repugnance. In particular, to take two developments that Buckley fought unsuccessfully to oppose, the Supreme Court has 'discovered' in the US Constitution both a right to abortion (part of an undefined 'right of privacy'), and a right to same-sex marriage.

One of the most important battles of the conservative movement in recent years has therefore been on behalf of the American Constitution, against those who would read into that brief document the rights and freedoms that appeal to modern liberals, but not, on the whole, those that appeal to conservatives (such as the right to life of the unborn child). Important in this battle has been Robert H. Bork (1927–2012), solicitor general and jurist, who argued that the duty of the judge is to construe the original intention of the Founders strictly, and not to import interpretations that reflect the judge's own desires and prejudices while being at variance with the letter and the spirit of the original document (*The Tempting of America*, 1990). Although there is latitude for disagreement, and the Constitution can be extrapolated to deal with circumstances that the Founders did not or could not foresee, all such extrapolation must be guided by respect for the overall intentions of the Constitution.

The habit of importing interpretations of constitutional clauses in order to satisfy this or that (usually liberal) prejudice is in fact tantamount to repudiating the Constitution entirely, and refusing to recognise it as setting limits to legislative and judicial powers. Moreover, it authorises judicial legislation in defiance of the will of

Congress and the elected representatives of the people. Therefore it is a violation of the democratic traditions of the American people. Bork was a particularly trenchant critic of the decision in *Roe* v. *Wade* (1973), legalising abortion. His more philosophical writings, in which he defended the spiritual and moral inheritance of America against modern corruption, placed him firmly in the conservative camp, a strong ally of Buckley and *National Review*. As a result, Bork's nomination to the Supreme Court by President Reagan in 1987 was so vehemently opposed by the liberal establishment that the appointment could not be confirmed by the Senate.

One other leading figure of the post-war conservative movement deserves mention here and that is Russell Kirk (1918–94), whose book *The Conservative Mind* (1953) was the first, and continuingly influential, attempt to define the conservative position as a comprehensive intellectual posture. Kirk assisted William Buckley in the founding of *National Review*, going on to establish his own journal, *Modern Age*, in 1957. Kirk attempts, in *The Conservative Mind*, to describe a unified movement – intellectual, political and cultural – in which the many conservative thinkers and politicians participate. Strongly influenced by Eliot, and also by Christian cultural conservatives such as C. S. Lewis and G. K. Chesterton, Kirk argued that both the ideas and the policies of the many who had reacted against liberal–socialist ideas in his time were anticipated by Burke, and also articulated by him in a way from which we could all learn. According to Gerald Russello, whose writings about Kirk are far clearer in this matter than Kirk himself,

Kirk's philosophy is founded in the following 'canons' or states of mind:

1. A belief in a transcendent order, which Kirk described variously as based in tradition, divine revelation or natural law;
2. An affection for the 'variety and mystery' of human existence;
3. A conviction that society requires orders and classes that emphasise 'natural' distinctions;
4. A belief that property and freedom are closely linked;
5. A faith in custom, convention, and prescription, and a recognition that innovation must be tied to existing traditions and customs, which entails a respect for the political value of prudence.

Those canons are not developed in any systematic way by Kirk, who preferred to range across the field of existing intellects, picking the flowers that attracted him. Indeed the Kirkean canons, detached from the philosophical arguments that might be used to justify them, have a somewhat commonplace air, and seem more like a wish list than a philosophy. Nevertheless, it is fair to say that Kirk set an example to generations of post-war Americans, young people especially, in presenting the conservative position as a common heritage, believable as a political doctrine, and also the inspiration for the highest artistic endeavours, as in the poetry of T. S. Eliot.

This is not to say that the philosophical heritage of conservatism has been ignored. The dispute over 'social justice', in which Hayek mapped out the territory, has broken out more recently in the American academy, following the magisterial work by the liberal John Rawls, *A Theory of Justice* (1970). Rawls's broad defence of a soft socialist position, according to which justice resides in the distribution of goods and advantages, rather than the actions of individuals, is backed up with elaborate arguments, drawing on game theory, moral philosophy and analytical metaphysics. The effect, if not the goal, has been to dazzle the ordinary conservative conscience. Conservatives have therefore left it to the libertarians to frame the response – notably the philosopher Robert Nozick who, in *Anarchy, State and Utopia* (1974), argues that theories of justice like that of Rawls, which define justice in terms of a pattern of distribution, will always infringe on freedom, and also run counter to the 'justice preserving transfers' which inform our everyday relations. The arguments here are complex, and continuing. But it is fair to say that American conservatives, in so far as they have noticed them, have nodded assent to the libertarian case.

This melding of the conservative and the libertarian standpoint can be witnessed in the multifaceted movement that arose in both Britain and America in the 1970s, and which has sometimes been referred to as the 'New Right', partly because it was, at the intellectual level at least, a response to the 'New Left' movement of the 1960s. The New Right movement was an intellectual companion to the Reagan–Thatcher alliance in politics, an attempt to reaffirm Western civic values in the face of Soviet aggression, and an unsystematic response to the Marxist and neo-Marxist

attempts to take over the academy. It was not so much ecumenical in the style of Buckley as diverse, being largely a
reaction, in Britain, to three decades of soft-socialist orthodoxy by a new generation of its exasperated victims.

One aspect, the defence of 'market solutions' to social
and political problems, grew into the approach to political
decision-making known now as 'neo-liberalism', and associated at first with the Chicago school of economic theory
and the 'public choice' theories developed in the University
of Virginia. Both schools pre-date the New Right movement, while providing it with a central core of economic
arguments. Important thinkers include Milton Friedman
in Chicago, whose *Capitalism and Freedom* (1962) became
a bible to American conservative think tanks during the
Presidency of Ronald Reagan, and James M. Buchanan
in Virginia, whose book, *The Calculus of Consent: Logical
Foundations of Constitutional Democracy* (1962), co-
authored with Gordon Tullock, attempts to give an explanation of the workings of democracy in purely economic
terms. Buchanan and others developed the theories of that
book into an account of the 'rent-seeking' behaviour of
bureaucracies, thereby debunking many of the exaggerated
claims made for the 'social justice' of the welfare state, and
providing a powerful response to the view that the market is
less compassionate than a socialist bureaucracy.

For a while neo-liberalism looked as though it was
taking off as a comprehensive political philosophy, endors-
ing the famous thesis of Joseph Alois Schumpeter (1882–
1950) in *Capitalism, Socialism and Democracy* (1942), that
the capitalist entrepreneur is the true instrument of positive

adaptation, sweeping aside all moribund habits and institutions in a storm of 'creative destruction'. However, the new economy, in which everything – marriage, family, art, faith and nation – was being marked up for sale in the global auction, caused widespread alarm as much on the right as on the left, with the result that today neo-liberalism is more often regarded as a threat to our inheritance than an important part of it.

Within the New Right, therefore, there has arisen another and countervailing tendency, which is the attempt to protect what matters, both from subversion by the socialist cult of equality and from dissolution under the impact of global forces, market forces included. This movement took off in Britain with the foundation of the *Salisbury Review*, under my editorship, in 1982. Named for the prime minister, the third Marquess of Salisbury (1830–1902), about whom little today is publicly known precisely because he wished to make only unnoticeable changes, the *Review* has taken a stance on behalf of national identity and traditional attachments against the emerging orthodoxy of 'multiculturalism'. It was also an important link during the 1980s between the New Right and the dissident movements in Eastern Europe, publishing letters and articles from the Czech, Polish and Hungarian underground, and emphasising that totalitarian communism was not an aberration within Marxism, but the condition towards which New Left ways of thinking were inevitably tending. However, its importance lay less in its confrontation with the neo-Marxist left than in its defence of British culture and institutions in the face of the challenge presented by mass migration.

Britain has seen the growth of Islamic communities that reject crucial aspects of the nation state. British schools have acquired the thankless task of integrating the children of these communities into a secular order that their parents denounce as blasphemous. And the left–liberal establishment has rushed forward to condemn as 'racist' any person – be it schoolteacher, social worker or journalist – who discusses in plain and truthful language what is happening to the social fabric of the country. These facts have defined a new agenda for conservatism, and one that the *Salisbury Review* adopted as its own in the 1980s, with adverse effects on the careers of its writers and its editor.

Indeed, all the old currents of opinion are apt to seem beside the point in our situation today, when the defence of Western civilisation is less a matter of confronting domestic resentment and socialist schemes for distributive justice, than of standing up to an armed and doctrinaire enemy, in the form of radical Islam. Once again conservatives and liberals stand side by side in defence of their shared goal, which is a society of free individuals, under a government that they themselves have chosen. But they live, now, in a world where free speech and free opinion are comprehensively threatened, where laughter is dangerous and where the fundamental assumptions of secular government are no longer shared by all those who enjoy its benefits.

Conservatives have therefore turned in a new direction, exploring the roots of secular government in the Christian inheritance, and the place of religion in a society which has made freedom of conscience into one of its ruling principles. The invention of the 'neo-conservative' label, to denote the political advisors and think tanks which have tried to turn American foreign policy towards a direct confrontation with despotic and Islamist movements in the wider world, is in part a recognition that conservatism, in so far as it now exists, is no longer about market economics and free trade, but about the wider global agenda.

Three thinkers typify the new movement of ideas: Samuel Huntington in America, Pierre Manent in France, and myself in Britain. We begin from very different premises. But we coincide in our belief that Muslim immigration poses a challenge to Western civilisation, and that the official policy of 'multiculturalism' is not a solution but part of the problem.

Samuel Huntington (1927–2008) was a political scientist known for his work on democratisation, who in later life addressed the new international situation following the collapse of communism. In *The Clash of Civilisations and the Making of World Order* (1996), he argued that the conflict of the cold war would be replaced by a violent and disorderly conflict between civilisations, as the Islamic world reacts to the global transfer of Western attitudes, Western technology and Western secularisation. This led him to raise, in *Who Are We?* (2002), the question of American identity. Written in the wake of the terrorist atrocities of 11 September 2001 (the 9/11 attacks on New York and Washington DC), the book argues that it will be impossible to respond in a coherent way to the Islamist threat without regaining confidence in our own identity. This means confidence not in our political institutions only, but in the spiritual inheritance on which they ultimately rest. The correct response to Islamist belligerence is, therefore, not simply the reaffirmation of the liberal order and the secular state. It is the rediscovery of ourselves, in a systematic policy of cultural conservatism.

Huntington's argument centres on what he calls the American Creed, which he believes to derive from the 'Anglo-Protestant' culture of the original settlers. And he marshals the evidence of recent historical scholarship, which sees the development of American political institutions, and the forging of the American national idea, as continuous with the Protestant 'Awakenings' that repeatedly swept across the continent. To separate this religious inheritance from the idea of America, to reconstitute as a purely secular body politic what began life as a sacred pledge, would be to deny the most vigorous input into the American experience.

The point, as Huntington sees it, is that civilisations cannot be defended merely by offering freedom and toleration. To offer toleration to those gripped by animosity to your way of life is to open the door to destruction. We must rediscover what we are and what we stand for, and having rediscovered it, be prepared to fight for it. That is now, as it has ever been, the conservative message. And what we stand for is a religious as much as a political inheritance.

Similar points are made by Pierre Manent in *La Situation de la France* (2015), a book also written in response to Islamist terrorism, in this case the murder of the editorial staff of the weekly magazine *Charlie Hebdo* in January 2015. Manent (b. 1949) is a professor of political philosophy at the École des Hautes Études en Sciences Sociales in Paris, and a co-founder of the quarterly journal *Commentaire*, which has been a major source of conservative thinking during the last three decades. Influenced by a reading of Leo Strauss (see Chapter 4), Manent has written extensively on the deeper meaning of Western civilisation, which he sees as continuous with the ancient city, defining and extending the condition of citizenship against both religious submission and imperial domination. In the modern context, Manent argues, we cannot expect Muslim citizens to submit whole-heartedly to the doctrine of 'human rights', as expounded by the original Declaration of the French revolutionaries. But we must, nevertheless, find a place for them in our society, which will respect their religious way of life. Hence we must offer them an object of loyalty that they can share with their fellow citizens. For Manent, this object of a shared loyalty can only be the nation, conceived as a spiritual inheritance under a rule of law. The transnational alternatives – Europe, the UN, the law of human rights, maybe the Islamic *ummah* itself – are either unappealing or run counter to the immediate and urgent need for the integration of the Muslim minority. Yet the governing elite has connived at the deliberate enfeeblement of the nation, adopting globalisation and the European project as the sole guides to the future, and believing that all Frenchmen could live as radical individuals, bound together by nothing more than the impartial law of the secular Republic.

Worse, there has been in official circles a deliberate silencing of discussion, a refusal to describe things by their proper names, and the adoption of the propaganda-word 'Islamophobia' to create a wholly imaginary enemy. As far as the official version of events is concerned, Islamist terrorism is a response to a continuous crime against the Muslim community – a crime committed by everyone who notices that Muslim customs are in friction with the traditional social order of France. The official propaganda passes over the fact that the Muslim community in France is financed and guided from outside – by the wealthy Wahhabite mission from Saudi Arabia, for example – and has no motive to regard France as the source and the object of its communal life. The European project only exacerbates the problem, since the integration of the Muslim community can only occur at the national level, where Muslims are represented by their vote, and not at the European level, where the people do not count.

Manent's subtle response to the question of Islam in France is also a deeply pondered examination of the French political and cultural inheritance, and a vindication of the national idea that had inspired the *renouveau catholique* described in Chapter 4. My own reflections, published in 2002 as *The West and The Rest,* and conceived following the terrorist attacks of 9/11, are an attempt to show the tension between traditional Sunni Islam and a man-made rule of law. I argue that there is a profound divide between a religious community, shaped by holy law and submission to a God who recognises neither national boundaries nor the rights of his opponents, and a political community, such as ours, in which there is legal opposition, man-made law, secular government, freedom of opinion, and representative institutions. The political community depends upon a pre-political loyalty, and I agree with Manent that this loyalty must be defined in national terms.

National loyalty means attachment to the territory that we share with our neighbours. It is the ground of the freedoms that we enjoy and which were announced and protected by the US Constitution. The political form of coexistence is a precious achievement and something to which conservatives, liberals and socialists ought all to be committed, and for which they should be prepared to pay the price. It is threatened both by Islamist intransigence, and by the culture of repudiation that prevails on the left, and which denounces every attempt to defend our inheritance as 'racist' or 'xenophobic'.

What is at stake, I argue, for both liberals and conservatives – and for socialists too, if they could permit themselves to think it – is the Western inheritance of citizenship, and the identity that goes with it. Here is how I put the point:

> Citizens enjoy rights – both the 'human rights' or 'natural rights' that are the pre-condition of their consent to be governed, and the right of participation in the political process. They are also bound by duties to their fellow citizens, and these duties spring from a peculiar experience of membership. Citizens are first and foremost members of a society of strangers, committed to the defence of their common territory and to the maintenance of the law that applies there. Citizenship therefore depends on pre-political loyalties of a territorial kind – loyalties rooted in a sense of the common home and of the trans-generational society that resides there. In short, citizenship as we know it depends on the nation, defined as a self-renewing organism clothed in the mantle of a law-governed state. (pp. 60–61)

Islam, by contrast, offers a pre-political loyalty that is defined without reference to territory, which denies religious freedom, and sees God, not politics, as the ultimate source of law. The confrontation with Islamic extremism, I conclude, 'requires a credible alternative to the absolutes with which the extremist conjures. It requires us not merely to believe in something, but to study how to put our beliefs into practice.' Like Manent, I look back to the spiritual inheritance of Christianity, and to the two great laws of Christ, who commanded us to love God entirely and to love our neighbour as ourselves. As he showed through his example and his parables, the neighbour is not the fellow believer, the family member, the fellow militant, but the one whom you come across: the one who, for whatever reason, is nearby. The nation state elevates neighbourhood and territory into the thing to which you belong. It is the means to reconcile people of different faiths and lifestyles, as they have been reconciled in America and would be reconciled in Europe too, were the elites to acknowledge that political representation is the solution to our current problems, and that representation is possible only on the assumption of a shared national identity. Our hope is that a form of Islam will emerge that accepts those truths, and which takes seriously the saying among Middle Eastern Muslims, *sabaHan man jama'naa* – all praise to the one we come across.

That position is a direct challenge to the habits of censorship and self-castigation that inform our public life. Now, as always, conservatives suffer under a burden of disapproval, which they believe comes from their habit of telling the truth, but which their opponents ascribe either to 'nostalgia' for an old and misremembered way of life or to a failure of compassion towards the new ways of life that are emerging to replace it. My own view is that conservatism will be a necessary ingredient in any solution to the emerging problems of today, and that the tradition of thinking that I have outlined in this book should therefore be part of the education of all politicians everywhere.

# FURTHER READING AND BIBLIOGRAPHY

The reader seeking a defence of conservatism in contemporary terms might care to look at my work *How to Be a Conservative*, London, Bloomsbury, 2014. The sources I have used include articles, reviews and works of literature not all of which merit citation in this bibliography. There follows a list of the major works on which I have drawn, their authors listed in alphabetical order, and, where convenient, available modern editions specified.

Arnold, Matthew, *Culture and Anarchy*, 1869; edited by Jane Garnett, Oxford, Oxford World's Classics, 2009

Bauer, Peter T. (Lord Bauer), *Dissent on Development*, Cambridge MA, Harvard UP, 1972

Bentham, Jeremy, *Introduction to the Principles of Morals and Legislation*, 1789; New York, Dover Philosophical Classics, 2007

Berry, Wendell, *The Unsettling of America*, 1977; reissued London, Avon Books, HarperCollins, 2015

Blackstone, Sir William, *Commentaries on the Laws of England*, 1765–69, edited by Wilfrid Prest, 4 vols, Oxford, OUP, 2016

Bloom, Allan, *The Closing of the American Mind*, New York, Simon & Schuster, 1987

Bork, Robert H., *The Tempting of America: Political Seduction of the Law*, New York, Touchstone, 1991

Buchanan, James M., and Tullock, Gordon, *The Calculus of Consent: Logical Foundations of Constitutional Democracy*, first appearing 1962 onwards, 3 vols, Liberty Foundation 1999

Buckley, William F. Jr, *God and Man at Yale: The Superstitions of Academic Freedom*, 1951; reissued, Washington DC, Regnery, 1977

Burke, Edmund, *Reflections on the Revolution in France*, 1790, in Edmund Burke, *Reflections on the Revolution in France and Other Writings* edited by Jesse Norman, London, Everyman Library, 2015

Burnham, James, *The Managerial Revolution: What is Happening in the World*, 1941; new edition New York, Praeger, 1972

Burnham, James, *The Struggle for the World*, 1947; reissued London, Forgotten Books, 2012

Burnham, James, *Suicide of the West: An Essay on the Meaning and Destiny of Liberalism*, 1964; reissued New York, Encounter Books, 2014

Carlson, Allan C., *The New Agrarian Mind: The Movement Toward Decentralist Thought in Twentieth-Century America*, New Brunswick, Transaction Books, 2000

Chambers, Whittaker, *Witness*, 1952; reissued Washington DC, Regnery, Cold War Classics, 2014

Chateaubriand, François-René, Vicomte de, *Génie du Christianisme*, 1802; *Genius of Christianity, or The Spirit and Beauty of the Christian Religion*, edited and translated by Charles I. White, Philadelphia, Murphy and Co., 1871 (reissued)

Chesterton, G. K., *Heretics*, 1905; reissued, various

Chesterton, G. K., *Orthodoxy*, 1908; reissued Teddington, Middlesex, The Echo Library, 2006

Chesterton, G. K., *The Everlasting Man*, 2010; reissued Martino Fine Books, 2010

Coleridge, Samuel Taylor, *On the Constitution of the Church and State, According to the Idea of Each*, 1830; reissued London, Forgotten Books, 2012

Cowling, Maurice, *Religion and Public Doctrine in Modern England*, 3 vols, Cambridge, CUP, 1980–2001

Disraeli, Benjamin, Earl of Beaconsfield, *Sybil, or The Two Nations*, 1845; edited by Sheila Smith, Oxford, OUP, Oxford World's Classics, 2008

Eliot, Thomas Stearns, *The Sacred Wood, Essays on Poetry and Criticism*, 1920, London, Faber and Faber; reissued 1997

Eliot, Thomas Stearns, *The Idea of a Christian Society*, 1939, London, Faber & Faber; reissued 1982

Friedman, Milton, *Capitalism and Freedom*, 1962; new edition Chicago, Chicago UP, 2002

Hamilton, Alexander, and Madison, James, *The Federalist Papers*, 1787–88, Oxford, Oxford World's Classics, 2008

Harrington, James, *The Commonwealth of Oceana* and *A System of Politics*, edited by J. G. A. Pocock, Cambridge University Press, 1992

Hayek, Friedrich von, *The Road to Serfdom*, 1944; London, Routledge Classics, 2001

Hayek, Friedrich von, *The Constitution of Liberty*, 1961; London, Routledge Classics, 2006

Hayek, Friedrich von, *Law, Legislation and Liberty*, 2 vols, London, Routledge, 1973, 1979

Hegel, G. W. F., *Phänomenologie des Geistes*, 1806; *Hegel's Phenomenology of Spirit*, edited by A. V. Miller, Oxford, OUP, 1976

Hegel, G. W. F., *Grundlinien der Philosophie des Rechts*, 1821; *Outlines of the Philosophy of Right*, edited and translated by T. M. Knox, Oxford, OUP, Oxford World's Classics, 2008

Herder, J. G. von, *Ideen zur Philosophie der Geschichte von Menschheit*, 1784–91; digested in F. M. Barnard, *Herder on Nationality, Humanity and History*, Toronto, McGill University Press, 2004

Hobbes, Thomas, *Leviathan*, 1651, edited by J. C. A. Gaskin, Oxford, Oxford World's Classics, 2008

Hooker, Richard, *Of the Laws of Ecclesiastical Polity*, from 1594, contained in *Works*, 3 vols, edited by John Keble, Oxford 1836

Hume, David, *The History of England*, 1744, 3-vol. Kindle edition available for free

Hume, David, *Essays – Moral, Political and Literary*, 1777, edited by Eugene F. Miller, New York, Cosimo Classics, 1987

Huntington, Samuel, *The Clash of Civilisations and the Remaking of the World Order*, New York, Free Press, 1996

Huntington, Samuel, *Who Are We? America's Great Debate*, New York, Free Press, 2002

Jefferson, Thomas, Declaration of Independence, 1776, and *Notes on the State of Virginia*, 1784, in *Jefferson: Political Writings*, edited by Joyce Oldham Appleby, Cambridge CUP, 1999

Kant, Immanuel, *Kant's Political Writings*, edited by H. S. Reiss, Cambridge, CUP, 1991

Kedoure, Elie, *Nationalism*, fourth edition, expanded, Oxford, Blackwell, 1993

Kedoure, Elie, *The Chatham House Version, and Other Middle Eastern Studies*, edited by David Pryce-Jones, Ivan R. Dee Inc., 2004

Kirk, Russell, *The Conservative Mind, from Burke to Eliot*, 1953; abridged edition, New York, Stellar Classics, 2016

Leavis, F. R., *New Bearings in English Poetry*, 1932; reissued London, Faber & Faber, 2008

Leavis, F. R., *Revaluation*, London Chatto and Windus, 1936; reissued Harmondsworth, Penguin Books, 1964

Leavis, F. R., *Education and the University*, London, Chatto and Windus, 1943; reissued Cambridge, CUP, 1979

Leavis, F. R., *The Great Tradition*, London, Chatto and Windus 1948; reissued Harmondsworth, Penguin, 1972

Lewis, C. S., *Mere Christianity*, 1952; reissued, London, William Collins, 2016

Locke, John, *Two Treatises of Civil Government*, 1690, edited by Peter Laslett, Cambridge, CUP, 1988

Maistre, Comte Joseph de, *Principe générateur des constitutions politiques*, 1809; *Generative Principle of Political Constitutions*, in *The Works of Joseph de Maistre*, edited and translated by Jack Lively, London, George Allen & Unwin, 1965

Maitland, Frederic William, *The Constitutional History of England: A Course of Lectures Delivered*, Cambridge, CUP, 1908

Manent, Pierre, *La Situation de la France*, Paris, Desclée de Brouwer, 2015

Mason, George, 'The Virginia Declaration of Rights', 1776, in Robert C. Mason, *George Mason of Virginia, Citizen, Statesman, Philosopher – Primary Source Edition*, Charleston, Nabu Press, 2013 (reissue)

Minogue, Kenneth, *The Servile Mind*, New York, Encounter Books, 2010

Montesquieu, Charles-Louis de Secondat, Baron de, *L'Esprit des lois*, 1734; *The Spirit of the Laws*, translated and edited by Anne M. Cohler, Cambridge, CUP, 1989

Nozick, Robert, *Anarchy, State and Utopia*, New York, Basic Books, 1974

Oakeshott, Michael, *Rationalism in Politics*, 1962; reissued *Rationalism in Politics and Other Essays*, edited by Timothy Fuller, Liberty Fund, 1991

Oakeshott, Michael, *On Human Conduct*, 1975; Oxford, Clarendon Press, 1991

Ortega y Gasset, José, *La deshumanización del arte*, 1925; *The Dehumanization of Art and Other Essays on Art, Culture, and Literature*, translated by Helene Weyl, Princeton, Princeton UP, 1968

Ortega y Gasset, José, *La rebelión de las masas*, 1930; *The Revolt of the Masses*, translated by anon, New York, Norton and Co., 1932

Orwell, George (Eric Blair), *Essays*, edited by Bernard Crick, Harmondsworth, Penguin Modern Classics, 2000

Paine, Thomas, *Rights of Man*, 1791–2, in *Rights of Man, Common Sense, and Other Political Writings*, Oxford, OUP, Oxford World's Classics, 2008

Rand, Ayn, *The Virtue of Selfishness*, 1964; Signet Edition, New York, 1992

Ransom, John Crowe, editor, *I'll Take My Stand: The South and the Agrarian Tradition*, 1930; reissued, Peter Smith Pub Inc., 1951

Rousseau, Jean-Jacques, *Du contrat social*, 1762; *The Social Contract*, introduction by Derek Matravers, Oxford, OUP, Classics of World Literature, 1998

Ruskin, John, *The Works of John Ruskin*, edited by Edward Tyas Cook, 39 vols, Cambridge, CUP; reissued 2010

Schumpeter, Joseph A., *Capitalism, Socialism and Democracy*, 1942; London, Routledge Classics, 2010

Scruton, Roger, *The West and the Rest, Globalisation and the Terrorist Threat*, London, Continuum, 2003

Smith, Adam, *The Theory of Moral Sentiments*, 1759, Harmondsworth, Penguin Classics, 2010

Smith, Adam, *An Inquiry into the Nature and Causes of the Wealth of Nations*, 1776, edited by Kathryn Sunderland as *The Wealth of Nations*, Oxford, OUP, Oxford World's Classics, 2008

Smith, Adam, *Lectures on Jurisprudence*, 1762–6, edited by Ronald L. Meek, Glasgow, Glasgow University Press, 1982

Stephen, Sir James Fitzjames, *Liberty, Equality, Fraternity*, 1873–4; Ann Arbor, University of Michigan, 1884; reissued, Literary Licencing LLC, 2014

Strauss, Leo, *The City and Man*, Charlottesville, University of Virginia Press, 1964

Tate, Allen, *Collected Poems*, New York, Farrar, Straus & Giroux Inc., 2007

Thoreau, Henry David, *Walden*, 1854; Harmondsworth, Pocket Penguin Edition, 2016

Tocqueville, Comte Alexis de, *De la démocratie en Amérique*, 1835; *Democracy in America and Two Essays on America*, edited by Isaac Kramnick, Harmondsworth, Penguin Classics, 2003

Tocqueville, Comte Alexis de, *L'ancien regime et la Révolution*, 1856; *The Old Regime and the Revolution*, edited by John Bonner, New York, Dover Books, 2010

Weaver, Richard, *Ideas Have Consequences*, Chicago, University of Chicago Press, 1948

Weil, Simone, *L'Enracinement: Prélude à une declaration des devoirs envers l'être humain*, 1949; *The Need for Roots: Prelude to a Declaration of Duties towards Mankind*; translated by Arthur Wills, with preface by T. S. Eliot, London, Routledge Classics, 2001

Weil, Simone, *La pesanteur et la grâce*, 1952; translated as *Gravity and Grace* by Emma Crawford and Marion von der Ruhr, with introduction by Gustave Thibon, new edition, London, Routledge, 2002